The Keto
Instant Pot Cookbook

A Practical Approach to the Ketogenic Diet with 200+ Easy Pressure Cooker Recipes

By Amanda Hodges

© Copyright 2017 by – Amanda Hodges - All rights reserved.

This document is geared towards providing exact and reliable information in regards to the topic and issue covered. The publication is sold with the idea that the publisher is not required to render accounting, officially permitted, or otherwise, qualified services. If advice is necessary, legal or professional, a practiced individual in the profession should be ordered.

- From a Declaration of Principles which was accepted and approved equally by a Committee of the American Bar Association and a Committee of Publishers and Associations.

In no way is it legal to reproduce, duplicate, or transmit any part of this document in either electronic means or in printed format. Recording of this publication is strictly prohibited and any storage of this document is not allowed unless with written permission from the publisher. All rights reserved.

The information provided herein is stated to be truthful and consistent, in that any liability, in terms of inattention or otherwise, by any usage or abuse of any policies, processes, or directions contained within is the solitary and utter responsibility of the recipient reader. Under no circumstances will any legal responsibility or blame be held against the publisher for any reparation, damages, or monetary loss due to the information herein, either directly or indirectly.

All data and information provided in this book is for informational purposes only. Amanda Hodges makes no representations as to accuracy, completeness, current, suitability, or validity of any information in this book & will not be liable for any errors, omissions, or delays in this information or any losses, injuries, or damages arising from its display or use. All information is provided on an as-is basis.

Respective authors own all copyrights not held by the publisher.

The information herein is offered for informational purposes solely, and is universal as so. The presentation of the information is without contract or any type of guarantee assurance.

The trademarks that are used are without any consent, and the publication of the trademark is without permission or backing by the trademark owner. All trademarks and brands within this book are for clarifying purposes only and are owned by the owners themselves, not affiliated with this document.

The author is not a licensed practitioner, physician or medical professional and offers no medical treatment, diagnoses, suggestions or counseling. The information presented herein has not been evaluated by the U.S Food & Drug Administration, and it is not intended to diagnose, treat, cure or prevent any disease. Full medical clearance from a licensed physician should be obtained before beginning or modifying any diet, exercise or lifestyle program, and physician should be informed of all nutritional changes. The author claims no responsibility to any person or entity for any liability, loss, damage or death caused or alleged to be caused directly or indirectly as a result of the use, application or interpretation of the information presented herein.

Table of Contents

Introduction

What is the Instant Pot?... 10
Perks of Cooking with the Instant Pot 11
All About the Ketogenic Diet.. 12
Health Benefits of 'Going Keto' 13
The Instant Pot and Ketogenic Eating 14

Breakfast Recipes

Scrambled Eggs with Ground Beef... 16
Italian Omelet with Herbs 17
Avocado Chicken with Spinach 18
Eggs with Spicy Marinara Sauce 19
Spicy Spinach with Eggs... 20
Creamy Raspberry Mug Cake 21
Beef Shiitake Bowl 22
Creamy Smoked Salmon 23
Asparagus with Cottage Cheese 24
Avocado Eggs Stir-Fry 25
Ground Beef with Steamed Cauliflower 26
Green Frittata 27
Avocado with Tomatoes... 28
Quick Pork with Mushrooms 29
Beef Kale Patties 30
Almond Bread in a Mug 31
Cinnamon Pancakes 32
Coconut Cherry Pancakes 33
Cheesy Eggs de Provence 34
Vichyssoise.. 35
Spring Vegetable Stew 36
Cottage Cheese Quiche 37
Bacon and Cheese Egg Bake 38

Curries and Indian Inspired Dishes

Chicken Biryani 40
Cauliflower Lamb Curry 41
Ginger Pork 42
Spicy Lamb 43
Eggplant Curry 44
Classic Ginger Curry 45
Tomato Rasam 46
Keto Sambar 47
Rajma Masala with Cauliflower 48
Keto Pav Bhaji 49
Paneer Butter Masala 50
Chicken Curry 51
Chili Tomato Stew 52
Coconut Turkey Curry 53
Butter Lamb Shoulder 54
Saffron Cauliflower Rice with Pork 55
Turmeric Chicken 56
Simple Palak Paneer 57
Indian Broccoli Shrimp 58
Spicy Lamb Coriander Curry 59
Tandoori Chicken 60
Simple Chicken Vindaloo 61

Seafood

Squid Rings with Potato and Spinach 64
Classic Fish Stew 65
Orange Glazed Salmon Fillets 66
Black Cauliflower Pasta 67
Wild Alaskan Salmon 68
Sweet Rosemary Cod Fillet 69
Tomato Shrimp Stew 70
Spicy Trout with Broccoli 71
King Prawn Stew with Avocado 72
Chili Hake Fillets 73
Mussel Chowder 74
Salmon Fillet with Dill 75
Wild Alaskan Cod with Cherry Tomatoes 76
Tiger Prawn Paella 77
Simple Squid Stew 78
Creamy Shrimp Stew 79
Salmon Steaks with Cheese 80
Sour King Scallops 81
Sweet Broccoli Fish Stew 82
5-Minute Mussels Soup 83
Lobster Tails in Butter Sauce 84
Steamed Mussels with Thyme 85

Poultry

Ginger Chicken with Vegetables 88
Cauliflower Turkey Risotto 89
Creamy Chicken Wings with Peppers 90
Balsamic Chicken Breast with Basil 91
Chicken Teriyaki 92
Moroccan Risotto 93
Chicken Fajitas 94
Keto Piccata 95
Chinese Simmered Chicken 96
Citrus Chicken Thighs 97
Cheesy Turkey 98
Cajun Chicken Breast 99
Shredded Chicken with Shiitake 100
Chicken Tostadas 101
Teriyaki Chicken Thighs with Peppers 102
Turkey Breast with Gorgonzola Sauce 103
Turkey Breast with Garlic Gravy 104
Simple Turkey Stew 105
Turkey Meatballs in Sweet Sauce 106
Turkey Leg with Garlic 107
Easy Turkey Roast 108
Chili Turkey Casserole 109

Beef & Lamb

Beef Egg Casserole 112
Italian Beef Chuck Roast 113
Rosemary Beef Roast 114
Chili Mushroom Beef Shank 115
Savory Cauliflower Beef Roast 116
Beef Steak in Balsamic Sauce 117
Chili Shoulder Roast 118
Grilled Beef Tenderloin 119
Creamy Shiitake Beef Sirloin 120
Marinated Beef Shank 121
Butter Beef Roast 122
Mediterranean Beef Meatballs 123
Pepper Short Ribs 124
Balsamic Fried Beef Roast 125
Beef Cremini 126
Beef Ragout 127
Creamy Beef Chili 128
Beef Brisket with Thyme Sauce 129
Beef with Greens 130
Quick Cheddar Beef Hash 131
Mustard Cheese Meatballs 132

Pork

Classic Meatloaf	134
Spicy Burgers	135
Garlic Pork Chops	136
Pork Steak in Mushroom Sauce	137
Rosemary Pork Shoulder	138
Balsamic Chops with Onions	139
Sweet Pork with Cauliflower	140
Pork Chops with Sauteed Peppers	141
Pork Shoulder with Sweet Potatoes	142
Sweet Garlic Pork	143
Pork Loin with Leeks	144
Easy Pork Ribs	145
Italian Roast	146
Chinese Pork Strips	147
Simple Tomato Pork Chops	148
Sweet Coconut Pork	149
Button Mushroom and Pepper Pork	150
Pork Neck with Sesame Seeds and Soy Sauce	151
Apple Cider Pork Ribs	152
Zucchini Pork	153
Steamed Pork Neck	154
Portobello Pork Butt	155
Pork Chops with Cheese and Prosciutto	156

Vegetables and Vegetarian Dishes

Cauliflower Broccoli Stir-Fry	158
Spinach Celery Stew	159
Creamy Collard Greens	160
Asparagus in Garlic Sauce	161
Cabbage Stew	162
Creamy Zucchini Soup	163
Swiss Chard Leek Stir-Fry	164
Creamy Bell Pepper Stew	165
Steamed Eggplant	166
Mushrooms with Asparagus	167
Spinach Cherry Tomato Hash	168
Garlic Bok Choy	169
Eggplant in Cream Chili Sauce	170
Broccoli with Parsley Cheese	171
Cauliflower Onion Hash	172
Brussels Sprouts with Mushrooms	173
Spinach Pepper Stew	174
Portobello Mushrooms in Lime Sauce	175
Basil Pesto Zucchini	176
Bell Peppers in Hot Sauce	177
Instant Keto Vegetarian Pizza	178

Stocks and Sauces

Basic Beef Stock 180
Lamb Stock with Celery 181
Basic Beef Stock with Bay Leaves. 182
Spring Fish Stock. 183
Chicken Vegetable Stock 184
Lamb Ribs Stock 185
Easy Chicken Stock 186
Spicy Pepper Beef Stock 187
Ginger Chicken Stock 188
Sour Onion Sauce 189
Classic Bolognese 190
Sweet BBQ Sauce 191
Tartare Sauce with Homemade Mayonnaise 192
Creamy Parsley Sauce 193
Spinach Sauce with Milk 194
Sour Garlic Sauce. 195
Instant Pot Marinara 196
Butter Sauce with Green Peppers 197
Tomato Onion Sauce 198
Dijon Sauce 199
Button Mushroom Sauce 200

Desserts

Easy Almond Brownies. 202
Creamy Vanilla Cake 203
Sweet Potato Cake 204
Mocha Brownies 205
Pumpkin Pie Bundt Cake 206
Classic Keto Cheesecake 207
Pecan Brownies. 208
Simple Vanilla and Chocolate Chips Cake 209
Chocolate Brownies with Orange Glaze 210
Quick Rum Cocoa Truffles 211
Raspberry Cheesecake 212
Chocolate Cake 213
Coconut Cocoa Brownies 214
Orange Lime Pudding 215
Almond Cocoa Spread 216
Chia Vanilla Custard 217
Walnut Pumpkin Mug Cake 218
Chocolate Cake with Vanilla Glaze 219
Rum Truffles 220
Mint Cake 221
Vanilla Cherry Panna Cotta 222
Mocha Pots de Creme. 223
Lemon Cake with Berry Syrup. 224
Easy Rum Cheesecake 225

Conclusion

Conclusion 228
Ketogenic Eating On-the-Go 229
The Ultimate Guide to Meal Prepping 230
The Family Ketogenic Diet 231
The Instant Pot + Ketogenic Eating: 232
Endless Possibilities! 232
Final Thoughts 233

Chapter 1
Introduction

What is the Instant Pot?

If you're reaching for this cookbook, chances are pretty good that you're either: 1) the proud owner of an Instant Pot pressure cooker or 2) considering adding one to your arsenal of kitchen gadgets. If you fall into the first category, congratulations! You're well on your way to embarking on a healthier lifestyle filled with delicious meals in a fraction of the time. If you're an Instant Pot newbie, listen up!

There has been a lot of buzz about the Instant Pot recently, and it's easy to see why! Unlike other kitchen appliances, the Instant Pot pressure cooker whips up your favorite dishes in no time at all. Whether you want to prepare something tasty for breakfast, a new cuisine from a faraway land for dinner, or a sweet dessert, your Instant Pot takes the pressure (and stress!) out of cooking.

So, how does the Instant Pot work its magic? Like all electric pressure cookers, the magic sauce is in the steam. As your pressure cooker warms up, steam levels begin to rise, and the overall pressure inside the cooker starts to increase. This rise in pressure actually increases the boiling point of water from an average 212° F to a whopping 250° F and, as a result, speeds up cooking time. In fact, most of the recipes we have included in this cookbook can be prepared in under 30 minutes!

By now, you're probably wondering what exactly sets the Instant Pot apart from traditional stovetop pressure cookers and even other electric models on the market. Well, unlike its stovetop cousins, the Instant Pot features an automatic timer that is specifically designed to keep you (and your kitchen!) safe. When you cook with an electric pressure cooker, you'll never face that dreaded, "Oh my gosh, did I leave the stove turned on?!" dilemma again. Why? These electric cookers are designed to automatically shut off when the steam levels rise to a certain point, keeping you (and your peace of mind) safe and intact!

Perks of Cooking with the Instant Pot

There's a reason the Instant Pot has become a household name within the past few years. Unlike other electric pressure cookers, the Instant Pot is packed with self-timed settings for just about any dish you can conjure up. From grass-fed meats to organic chicken, whole grain rice, organic soups, veggie dishes, side dishes, and everything in between, your Instant Pot likely has a setting for it!

Another great perk to Instant Pot cooking is the all-in-one functionality of this nifty little device. Gone are the days when you needed a separate rice cooker, slow cooker, pressure cooker, browning pan, and skillet; your Instant Pot is designed to replace them all, saving you loads of space. Trust us; your kitchen cabinets will thank you!

The Instant Pot is also a green and eco-friendly option making it an ideal mate with your Ketogenic Diet. Since it uses up to 70% less energy, you are doing Mother Earth a favor every time you switch on your Instant Pot. Another big plus? The Instant Pot is made entirely of stainless steel so you can kiss those nasty chemical linings "Good Bye!" for good. After all, you don't want to spoil that tasty farm-to-table healthy meal of yours with harsh chemicals!

Last but certainly not least, let's talk styles and specs. Unlike other electric pressure cookers out there, the Instant Pot comes in 5 different models in a variety of sizes so you can tailor your cooking experience to your unique needs. Whether you need to whip up dinner for a family of 12, a scrumptious meal for 1, or a romantic dessert for 2, there is an Instant Pot model for you! The best part? Instant Pot offers models that span the entire low-tech/high-tech spectrum. Looking for a tech-savvy pressure cooker that hooks up to your smartphone? Check. Need something a little less intimidating? There's an Instant Pot with that too!

All About the Ketogenic Diet

For the last 20 years, it seems as though we've created a fad diet for nearly everything. We've dabbled in diets that eliminate fat, regimes that promote protein-loading, lemon water cleanses, fish-only diets, "no red meat" diets, diets that frown upon gluten, smoothie-only diets...we really have seen it all. But have you ever asked yourself where the science is supporting any of these fad diets or if they even work?

If you're one of the millions of people on this planet that have tried a fad diet only to be met with disappointment, you know what we're talking about. Well, just like your mother always told you, if it seems too good to be true, it probably is! Fad diets like this often lack any sort of real scientific backing, and are a recipe for frustration when, 60-days in, you step on the scale only to discover you've actually gained 15 pounds!

Luckily, the Ketogenic Diet is different. Unlike fad diets or other unsubstantiated eating crazes, a Keto diet is rooted in your body's own innate food processing system. By cutting down carbohydrates or sugar and increasing consumption of healthy fats, your body goes into a natural state that breaks down stored fat. Still a skeptic? Let's break it down:

- When you eat a diet that is rich in carbohydrates and sugar, your body begins to produce glucose and insulin for a quick supply of energy.
- Since your body can sustain itself on glucose and insulin alone, there is no need to tap into fat storage supplies which, over time, build up.
- Conversely, when you decrease consumption of carbohydrates, your body goes into a natural state called "Ketosis."
- During Ketosis, your liver begins to produce ketones that break down fats stored throughout the body.
- Remember, you aren't starving your body with a Keto diet; you're eliminating quickly digestible compounds like sugars and carbohydrates.
- In other words, your body's own source of stored nutrients and energy are utilized instead of those quick-fix carbohydrates!

When you eat a Keto diet, your body returns to a more natural state (you know, the one we enjoyed in the days before instant Mac n' Cheese or microwave popcorn). Over time, you can actually train your body to process foods more efficiently and, in the process, cut down unwanted fat. The end result? A truly healthy lifestyle that helps you lose (and keep off!) those extra pounds for good!

Health Benefits of 'Going Keto'

Along with its obvious weight-reducing qualities, some research suggests that a Ketogenic Diet helps those suffering from diabetes control their blood sugar. It has been particularly beneficial for people with Type II Diabetes or Pre-Diabetes since the entire diet is based on the concept of limiting (and controlling!) sugars!

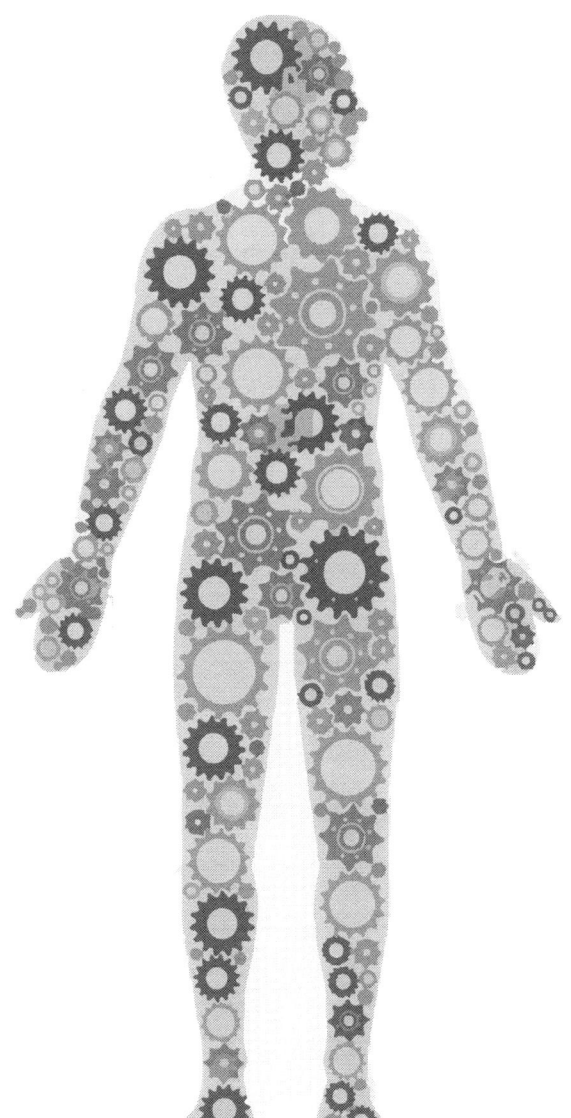

The Ketogenic Diet has also been found to increase focus and mental clarity which, when you think about it, makes a whole lot of sense. Ever experienced a nasty case of "food coma" after binging on that extra-large pizza or the heaped serving of spaghetti? Scientifically, these quick-absorb sources of energy are not enough to sustain brain function (hence the foggy feeling) and often leave us feeling...blah. A Keto diet, on the other hand, is rich in slow-absorbing ketones and nutrients that feed our brain all day long!

Another perk of going Keto? Increased energy! When your body slowly absorbs energy (as opposed to the quick pick-me-up that candy bar supplies), you avoid the horrible crash a mere hour or two later. This is particularly important when you lead a busy lifestyle, workout often, or are just a regular "on the go!" type of guy or gal, and need to sustain energy regardless of how many meetings, emails, soccer games, or date nights life may throw your way!

The Instant Pot and Ketogenic Eating

If kitchen appliances and diets could create online dating profiles, these two would surely "swipe right" for one another! In many ways, the Instant Pot pressure cooker and the Ketogenic Diet are a match made in heaven. After all, the Instant Pot delights in preparing healthy, hearty meals for your entire family while the Ketogenic Diet promotes a healthy, sustainable lifestyle.

For many people, the biggest deterrent from cooking healthy meals is time. In fact, most of the generic Ketogenic Diet cookbooks on the market require you to spend hours upon hours with food prepping (and really, who has time for that?!). When you pair the Ketogenic Diet with the Instant Pot though, you truly get the best of both worlds; a diet that is rich in the nutrients and ketones your body craves, without the unnecessary prep time or unwanted hassle.

Put it this way: if you could enjoy a healthy and wholesome meal in less time than it takes to hop in your car and head to the drive-thru, would you do it? If you could prepare a delicious meal that starved off cravings and helped you lose weight, would you try it? If you could feed your body the healthy fats and proteins it deserves without spending hours upon hours with food prepping, would you give it a go? Well, what's stopping you? Let's get started!

Chapter 2

Breakfast Recipes

Scrambled Eggs with Ground Beef

(TotalTime: 20 MIN| Serves: 2)

Ingredients:

For eggs:
- 7 oz ground beef
- 1 onion, finely chopped
- 3 eggs
- ¼ cup milk
- ¼ cup fresh goat's cheese

Spices:
- 1 tsp garlic powder
- ¼ tsp rosemary powder
- 1 tbsp tomato paste
- ½ tsp sea salt
- 2 tbsp olive oil

Directions:

1. Plug in the instant pot and grease the stainless steel insert with olive oil. Press the "Sauté" button and add onions. Stir-fry until translucent. Now, add beef and tomato paste. Continue to cook for 5 more minutes, stirring occasionally.
2. Meanwhile, whisk together eggs, milk, goat's cheese, rosemary powder, garlic powder, and salt. Pour the mixture into the pot and stir slowly with a wooden spatula. Cook until slightly underdone.
3. Remove from the heat and serve.

Per Serving:
(Calories 483| Total Fats 31g | Net Carbs: 6.3g | Protein 43.1g |Fiber: 1.2g)

Breakfast Recipes

Italian Omelet with Herbs

(TotalTime: 20 MIN | Serves: 2)

Ingredients:

For omelet:
- ½ medium-sized tomato, chopped
- 3 large eggs
- 2 garlic cloves, crushed

Spices:
- 2 tbsp olive oil
- ½ tsp sea salt
- 1 tsp Italian seasoning mix

Directions:

1. Grease the inner pot with two tablespoons of olive oil and press the "Sauté" button. Heat up and add tomatoes. Cook for 2-3 minutes, stirring constantly.
2. Now add garlic and season with Italian seasoning mix. Continue to cook for another 1-2 minute. Remove from the pot and transfer to a bowl. Set aside.
3. Meanwhile, in a small bowl, whisk the eggs together. Pour the mixture in the pot and continue to cook for 2-3 minutes or until set.
4. Press the "Cancel" button and gently remove the inner pot. Using a wooden spatula, loosen the edges and remove the eggs.
5. Add tomatoes and fold over. Serve immediately.

Per Serving:
(Calories 235 | Total Fats 21.5g | Net Carbs: 1.9g | Protein 9.8g | Fiber: 0.3g)

Breakfast Recipes

Avocado Chicken with Spinach

(TotalTime: 50 MIN| Serves: 3)

Ingredients:

- 7 oz boneless and skinless chicken breast, chopped into bite-sized pieces
- 1 cup fresh spinach, chopped
- 1 large leek, finely chopped
- 1 cup avocado chunks
- 1 small onion, finely chopped
- 1 garlic clove, crushed
- 1 cup cottage cheese
- 3 tbsp butter

Spices:
- 1 tsp salt
- ½ tsp dried rosemary

Directions:

1. Plug in the instant pot and press the "Sauté" button. Grease the inner pot with butter and heat up. Add chicken and sprinkle with salt. Cook for 12-15 minutes, stirring occasionally.
2. Now add avocado and continue to cook for 5 minutes. If necessary, add more olive oil.
3. Finally, add onions, garlic, and chopped leeks. Give it a good stir and cook until completely soft.
4. Add spinach and sprinkle with rosemary. Press the "Cancel" button and cover with the lid. Let it sit for 10 minutes.
5. Remove from the pot and transfer to a deep bowl. Stir in the cottage cheese and serve immediately.

Per Serving:
(Calories 382g | Total Fats 24.5g | Net Carbs: 5.8g | Protein 31.2g |Fiber: 4g)

Breakfast Recipes

Eggs with Spicy Marinara Sauce

(TotalTime: 20 MIN| Serves: 3)

Ingredients:

For omelet:
- 5 large eggs
- ½ onion, finely chopped
- 2 garlic cloves, minced
- 1 red bell pepper, diced
- 2 cup cherry tomatoes
- 2 tbsp olive oil

Spices:
- 1 tsp salt
- ½ tsp smoked paprika
- ½ tsp cumin powder
- ¼ tsp freshly ground black pepper
- 1 tsp chili powder
- 1 tbsp dried parsley

Directions:

1. Grease the bottom of the stainless steel insert with oil and press the SAUTE button. Heat the oil and add diced onion, garlic cloves, and diced red bell pepper. Season with chili powder, paprika, salt, pepper, and cumin. Stir well and cook for 5 minutes, or until translucent and soft.
2. Add tomatoes and give it a good stir. Press the CANCEL button and chill for another 5 minutes.
3. In a medium-sized bowl, separate egg whites from yolks. Pour the egg whites into the pot and stir gently with a wooden spoon or a spatula.
4. Close the lid and set the steam release handle to the SEALING position. Press the Manual button and set the timer for 1 minute on LOW pressure.
5. When you hear the end signal, press the CANCEL button and move the pressure valve to the VENTING position to release the pressure. Open the lid and transfer the mixture to a serving plate.
6. Optionally, sprinkle with some chopped parsley or season with some smoked paprika.

Per Serving:
(Calories 244 | Total Fats 18g | Net Carbs: 8.3g | Protein 12.3g | Fiber: 2.4g)

Spicy Spinach with Eggs

(Total Time: 25 MIN | Serves: 4)

Ingredients:

- 2 lbs spinach, chopped
- 5 large eggs
- 1 cup vegetable stock
- ¼ cup Parmesan cheese, grated
- 1 small chili pepper, finely chopped

Spices:
- 1 tsp onion powder
- ¼ tsp garlic powder
- ¼ tsp chili powder
- 1 tsp salt
- ¼ tsp cayenne pepper

Directions:

1. Rinse the spinach under cold running water using a large colander. Drain and chop into small pieces.
2. Plug in the instant pot and place the spinach in the stainless steel insert. Pour in the vegetable broth and 1 cup of water. Sprinkle with some salt and close the lid.
3. Set the steam release handle and press the "Manual" button. Set the timer for 5 minutes and cook on "High" pressure.
4. When done, perform a quick release of the pressure and open the pot. Press the "Saute" button and chili pepper. Sprinkle with garlic powder, onion powder, chili powder, salt, and cayenne pepper. Give it a good stir and cook for 5 minutes, or until the liquid is reduced by half.
5. Poach the eggs on top of the spinach and sprinkle all with parmesan cheese.
6. Turn off the pot and transfer all to a serving dish.
7. Enjoy!

Per Serving:
(Calories 169 | Total Fats 8.7g | Net Carbs: 4.7g | Protein 16.8g | Fiber: 5.3g)

Creamy Raspberry Mug Cake

(Total Time: 10 MIN | Serves: 3)

Ingredients:

- 4 large eggs
- ½ cup cream cheese
- ½ cup heavy whipping cream
- ½ cup almond flour
- ½ tsp baking powder
- ¼ cup fresh raspberries

Spices:
- ¼ tsp powdered stevia
- ¼ tsp vanilla extract

Directions:

1. In a large mixing bowl, combine eggs, cream cheese, almond flour, and baking powder. With a whisking attachment on, beat until well combined and smooth.
2. Pour the mixture into oven-safe mugs and set aside.
3. Plug in your instant pot and pour 1 cup of water in the stainless steel insert. Position a trivet and place mugs on top.
4. Securely lock the lid and adjust the steam release handle. Press the "Manual" button and set the timer for 3 minutes. Cook on "High" pressure.
5. Meanwhile, combine heavy whipping cream with powdered stevia and vanilla extract. Beat until combined and set aside.
6. When you hear the cooker's end signal, perform a quick release of the pressure by moving the valve to the "Venting" position. Open the pot and transfer the mugs to a wire rack using oven mitts.
7. Top each mug with raspberry cream and serve immediately.
8. Enjoy!

Per Serving:
(Calories 418 | Total Fats 36.5g | Net Carbs: 5.1g | Protein 15.8g | Fiber: 2.7g)

Breakfast Recipes

Beef Shiitake Bowl

(TotalTime: 20 MIN| Serves: 4)

Ingredients:

- 8 oz ground beef
- 1 cup Shiitake mushrooms, sliced
- 4 large eggs, beaten
- 1 small onion, chopped
- ½ medium-sized avocado, sliced
- ¼ cup olives, pitted
- 1 tbsp extra virgin olive oil

Spices:
- 1 tsp smoked paprika, ground
- 1 tsp salt
- 1 tsp black pepper

Directions:

1. Plug in your instant pot and grease the stainless steel insert with olive oil. Press the "Sauté" button and add onions and beef. Cook for 5 minutes, stirring occasionally.
2. Add mushrooms and avocado. Sprinkle with smoked paprika, salt, and pepper. Stir well and add ½ cup of water. Close the lid and adjust the steam release handle. Press the "Manual" button and set the timer for 5 minutes. Cook on "High" pressure.
3. When done, perform a quick release of the pressure by turning the valve to the "Venting" position. Open the lid and stir in the eggs and olives. Press the "Sauté" button and cook for 2-3 minutes more.
4. Turn off the pot and transfer all to serving bowls.
5. Serve immediately.

Per Serving:
(Calories 297 | Total Fats 18g | Net Carbs: 7g | Protein 24.9g |Fiber: 3.4g)

Creamy Smoked Salmon

(TotalTime: 15 MIN | Serves: 2)

Ingredients:

- 2 oz smoked salmon, cut into bite-sized pieces
- 2 large eggs, beaten
- 1 tsp olive oil
- ¼ tsp dried thyme

For the creamy sauce:
- ½ cup almond milk, unsweetened
- ¼ cup walnuts, chopped
- ½ cup spinach, chopped
- 1 tsp sea salt
- ½ tsp black pepper, ground
- 1 tbsp lemon juice, freshly squeezed

Directions:

1. Combine almond milk, walnuts, and spinach in food processor. Blend until well combined and add salt, pepper, and lemon juice. Blend again for 1 minute and set aside.
2. Plug in your instant pot and grease the stainless steel insert with some olive oil. Add salmon pieces and eggs. Sprinkle with thyme and cook for 3 minutes. Using a large spatula, remove the omelet from the pot. Set aside covered.
3. Now, add the previously blended sauce mixture to the pot. Close the lid and adjust the steam release handle. Press the "Manual" button and set the timer for 3 minutes. When done, perform a quick release of the pressure and open the pot.
4. Transfer the omelet to a serving plate and drizzle with hot sauce.
5. Serve immediately.

Per Serving:
(Calories 365 | Total Fats 32.2g | Net Carbs: 3.3g | Protein 16.9g | Fiber: 2.8g)

Asparagus with Cottage Cheese

(TotalTime: 25 MIN | Serves: 2)

Ingredients:

- 1 cup asparagus, trimmed and chopped
- ½ cup cottage cheese, crumbled
- 2 tbsp Greek yogurt, full-cream
- 4 large eggs, beaten
- 2 garlic cloves, finely chopped
- 1 tbsp olive oil

Spices:
- 1 tsp salt
- ¼ tsp chili pepper, ground
- 2 tsp balsamic vinegar
- ¼ tsp black pepper, ground

Directions:

1. Rinse the asparagus under cold running water and trim off the woody ends. Cut into bite-sized pieces and set aside.
2. Plug in your instant pot and pour one cup of water in the stainless steel insert. Position a trivet on the bottom and place a steam basket on top. Add the asparagus and sprinkle with some salt. Close the lid and adjust the steam release handle.
3. Press the "Steam" button and set the timer for 10 minutes.
4. When done, perform a quick release of the pressure and open the pot. Remove the steam basket and water from the pot and wipe with a kitchen paper.
5. Now, add olive oil to the stainless steel insert and press the "Sauté" button. Add garlic and cook for 1 minute. Add eggs, cheese, and yogurt. Sprinkle with chili, salt, and pepper. Cook for 3-4 minutes, or until eggs are set. Turn off the pot.
6. Transfer the asparagus to a serving plate and top with cheesy mixture.
7. Serve immediately.

Per Serving:
(Calories 289 | Total Fats 18.6g | Net Carbs: 5.9g | Protein 24.1g | Fiber: 1.6g)

Breakfast Recipes

Avocado Eggs Stir-Fry

(TotalTime: 15 MIN| Serves: 2)

Ingredients:

- 1 medium-sized avocado, pitted and cubed
- 2 large eggs, beaten
- 2 tbsp green onions, finely chopped
- 1 tsp olive oil
- 1 tbsp butter

Spices:
- ½ tsp sea salt
- ¼ tsp black pepper, ground
- ¼ tsp red chili flakes

Directions:

1. Peel the avocado and cut in half. Remove the pit and cut into bite-sized cubes. Set aside.
2. Plug in your instant pot and melt the butter in the stainless steel insert. Press the "Sauté" button and add avocado cubes. Sprinkle with salt and pepper and cook for 3-4 minutes, stirring occasionally.
3. Now, add eggs, green onions, and olive oil to taste. Optionally, add 2 tablespoons of milk for a creamier texture.
4. Cook for 3 more minutes, or until the eggs are set. Press the "Cancel" button and turn off the pot. Transfer all to serving plate and optionally, top with some heavy cream or plain Greek yogurt.
5. Enjoy!

Per Serving:
(Calories 350 | Total Fats 32.7g | Net Carbs: 2.6g | Protein 8.4g |Fiber: 7g)

Breakfast Recipes

Ground Beef with Steamed Cauliflower

(TotalTime: 20 MIN| Serves: 2)

Ingredients:

- 8 oz ground beef
- 2 medium-sized bell pepper, chopped
- 1 cup cauliflower, chopped
- 1 tbsp butter
- 2 tbsp heavy cream
- 1 tbsp chives, finely chopped

Spices:
- ½ tsp dried thyme, ground
- ¼ tsp red chili flakes
- ½ tsp sea salt
- ¼ tsp black pepper, ground
- ¼ tsp smoked paprika, ground

Directions:

1. Plug in your instant pot and add the butter in the stainless steel insert. Press the "Sauté" button and add ground beef. Sprinkle with some salt, pepper, and smoked paprika. Cook for 5 minutes, or until golden brown. Stir occasionally.
2. Add bell peppers and heavy cream. Give it a good stir and cook for 2 more minutes. Press the "Cancel" button and stir in the chives immediately. Let it stand for 5 minutes and then transfer to a serving dish.
3. Now, clean the stainless steel insert and fill with 1 cup of water. Position a trivet on the bottom. Place the cauliflower in the steam basket and set the basket on the top of a trivet. Seal the lid and adjust the steam release handle.
4. Press the "Steam" button and set the timer for 10 minutes. Cook on "High" pressure. When done, perform a quick release and open the lid. Sprinkle with chili flakes and optionally, with some olive oil for better taste.
5. Serve steamed cauliflower with previously prepared ground beef.

Per Serving:
(Calories 366 | Total Fats 18.8g | Net Carbs: 9.4g | Protein 37.1g |Fiber: 3.1g)

Green Frittata

(Total Time: 20 MIN | Serves: 4)

Ingredients:

- 1 lb celery stalks, chopped
- 1 cup fresh spinach, chopped
- 1 cup fresh kale, chopped
- 6 large eggs
- 1 cup cheddar cheese, grated
- 2 tbsp butter
- 1 tbsp extra virgin olive oil
- 2 garlic cloves, minced

Spices:
- 1 tsp sea salt
- 1 tsp black pepper, freshly ground
- 1 tsp Italian seasoning
- ½ tsp onion powder

Directions:

1. Combine all greens in a large colander and rinse thoroughly under running water. Drain and chop into bite-sized pieces. Set aside.
2. Plug in the instant pot and add butter to the stainless steel insert. Press the "Saute" button and gently melt, stirring with a wooden spatula.
3. Add garlic and cook for 2 minutes. Now, add celery, spinach and kale. Cook for 5 minutes, or until wilted.
4. Crack the eggs on top and stir once to combine with greens. Sprinkle with salt, pepper, Italian seasoning, and onion powder. Top with cheddar cheese and cook for 3-4 minutes more, or until the eggs are set.
5. Turn off the pot and transfer the frittata to a serving plate. Drizzle with olive oil and serve immediately.
6. Enjoy!

Per Serving:
(Calories 338 | Total Fats 26.7g | Net Carbs: 5.1g | Protein 18.2g | Fiber: 2.4g)

Avocado with Tomatoes

(Total Time: 15 MIN | Serves: 3)

Ingredients:

- 1 ripe avocado, peeled, pitted, and cubed
- 1 cup tomatoes, diced
- ½ cup heavy cream
- 1 small onion, chopped
- 2 tbsp fresh parsley, chopped
- ½ cup green onions, chopped
- 1 tbsp olive oil
- 1 tbsp lemon juice

Spices:
- 1 tsp sea salt
- 1 tsp black pepper, ground
- ½ tsp dried oregano, ground
- ½ tsp dried thyme, ground
- ¼ tsp dried marjoram, ground

Directions:

1. Peel the avocado and cut in half. Remove the pit and cut into bite-sized pieces. Set aside.
2. Plug in the instant pot and grease the stainless steel insert. Press the "Saute" button and add onions and avocado. Cook for 3-4 minutes, stirring occasionally.
3. Now, add tomatoes, heavy cream, parsley, and green onions. Sprinkle with salt, pepper, oregano, thyme, and marjoram. Give it a good stir and securely lock the lid.
4. Set the steam release handle and press the "Manual" button. Set the timer for 5 minutes and cook on "High" pressure.
5. When you hear the cooker's end signal, perform a quick pressure release and open the pot.
6. Stir in the lemon juice and transfer all to a serving dish.
7. Serve warm.

Per Serving:
(Calories 276 | Total Fats 25.4g | Net Carbs: 6.5g | Protein 3g | Fiber: 6.6g)

Breakfast Recipes

Quick Pork with Mushrooms

(TotalTime: 20 MIN | Serves: 2)

Ingredients:

- 10 oz pork, minced
- 6 oz button mushrooms, sliced
- 1 small zucchini, chopped
- 1 small onion, finely chopped
- 1 tbsp Dijon mustard
- 1 tbsp olive oil

Spices:
- ¼ tsp dried basil, ground
- ¼ tsp garlic powder
- ½ tsp salt
- ½ tsp black pepper, ground

Directions:

1. Plug in your instant pot and add the olive oil in the stainless steel insert. Press the "Sauté" button and add onions. Stir-fry for 2-3 minutes and add minced pork. Sprinkle with garlic powder, salt, and pepper. Give it a good stir and cook for 3-4 minutes, or until browned.
2. Add zucchini and mushrooms. Pour 1 cup of water and close the lid. Adjust the steam release handle and press the "Manual" button. Set the timer for 6 minutes and cook on "High" pressure.
3. When you hear the cooker's end signal, perform a quick release of the pressure by turning the valve to the "Venting" position. Open the pot and press the "Sauté" button.
4. Stir in the Dijon mustard and sprinkle with dried thyme. Transfer to a serving plate and enjoy!

Per Serving:
(Calories 312 | Total Fats 12.7g | Net Carbs: 6.4g | Protein 41.3g | Fiber: 2.7g)

Beef Kale Patties

(TotalTime: 25 MIN | Serves: 4)

Ingredients:

- 1 lb ground beef
- 1 cup fresh kale, finely chopped
- 1 large egg, beaten
- 1 tbsp almond flour
- 1 tbsp olive oil

Spices:
- ½ tsp dried rosemary, ground
- ½ tsp dried oregano, ground
- 1 tsp sea salt
- ½ tsp black pepper, ground

Directions:

1. Rinse well the kale under cold running water using a large colander. Drain and finely chop. Set aside.
2. In a large mixing bowl, combine ground beef, kale, egg, and flour. Mix with your hands until well incorporated. Add flour and all spices. Mix again until smooth mixture. Shape about 8 patties, approximately 2-inch in diameter.
3. Grease a fitting springform pan with some olive oil. Add the patties and set aside.
4. Plug in your instant pot and pour 1 cup of water in the stainless steel insert. Position a trivet on the bottom and place the pan on top. Securely lock the lid and adjust the steam release handle. Press the "Manual" button and set the timer for 15 minutes. Cook on "High" pressure.
5. When done, perform a quick release of the pressure and open the pot. Remove the pan from the pot using oven mitts. Place on a wire rack and cool completely.
6. Optionally, brown the patties on "Sauté" mode for 1 minute on both sides.

Per Serving:
(Calories 279 | Total Fats 12.7g | Net Carbs: 1.9g | Protein 36.9g | Fiber: 0.7g)

Breakfast Recipes

Almond Bread in a Mug

(TotalTime: 25 MIN | Serves: 3)

Ingredients:

- 1 cup almond flour
- ½ cup minced almonds
- 2 large eggs, beaten
- 3 tbsp coconut oil, melted
- 1 tsp baking powder

Spices:
- ½ tsp salt
- ¼ tsp cinnamon, ground
- ½ tsp powdered stevia

Directions:

1. In a large mixing bowl, combine almond flour, baking powder, minced almonds, salt, cinnamon, and stevia. Stir with a kitchen spatula until well incorporated. Add eggs and coconut oil. With a paddle attachment on, beat until all well combined.
2. Pour the mixture into the oven-safe mugs, about 1/3 of a mug. Set aside.
3. Plug in your instant pot and pour 1 cup of water in the stainless steel insert. Position a trivet on the bottom and place the mugs on top. Cover with lid and adjust the steam release handle. Press the "Manual" button and set the timer for 4 minutes. Cook on "High" pressure.
4. When done, release the pressure naturally. Open the pot and let it chill for a while.
5. Using oven mitts carefully transfer the mugs to a wire rack. Let it cool completely before serving.

Per Serving:
(Calories 362 | Total Fats 31.9g | Net Carbs: 4.8g | Protein 11.7g | Fiber: 4.6g)

Cinnamon Pancakes

(TotalTime: 20 MIN | Serves: 3)

Ingredients:

- 1 cup almond flour
- 2 large eggs
- ½ tsp baking powder
- 1 tbsp coconut butter, melted
- 2 tbsp milk

Spices:
- 1 tsp cinnamon, ground
- ½ tsp powdered stevia
- ½ tsp vanilla extract

Directions:

1. In a large mixing bowl, combine almond flour, baking powder, cinnamon, and stevia. Using a kitchen spatula, mix until combined.
2. Now, add eggs, vanilla extract, and milk. With a whisking attachment on, beat until smooth batter.
3. Plug in your instant pot and grease the stainless steel insert with coconut butter. Pour about 1/3 of the mixture into the pot and securely lock the lid. Adjust the steam release handle and press the "Manual" button. Set the timer for 5 minutes and cook on "High" pressure.
4. When done, perform a quick release of the pressure and open the pot. Carefully remove the pancake to a serving plate. Repeat the process with the remaining batter.
5. Serve pancakes with some fresh raspberries.

Per Serving:
(Calories 312 | Total Fats 24.3g | Net Carbs: 5.7g | Protein 12.9g | Fiber: 5.3g)

Breakfast Recipes

Coconut Cherry Pancakes

 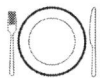

(TotalTime: 20 MIN | Serves: 3)

Ingredients:

- 1 cup almond flour
- 1 tsp baking powder
- ½ cup cream cheese, softened
- 3 large eggs, beaten
- 2 tbsp coconut milk
- 1 tbsp coconut butter, melted

Spices:
- 1 tsp powdered stevia
- 1 tsp cherry extract
- ¼ tsp nutmeg, ground

Directions:

1. In a large mixing bowl, combine coconut flour, baking powder, stevia, and nutmeg. Stir well using a kitchen spatula. Now, add eggs, cream cheese, coconut milk, nutmeg and cherry extract. With a whisking attachment on, beat until smooth and creamy.
2. Plug in your instant pot and grease the stainless steel insert with coconut butter. Pour about 1/3 of the mixture and securely lock the lid. Adjust the steam release handle and press the "Manual" button. Set the timer for 5 minutes and cook on "High" pressure.
3. When you hear the cooker's end signal, perform a quick release of the pressure by moving the valve to the "Venting" position. Open the pot and repeat the process with the remaining batter.
4. Top with some plain yogurt and sprinkle with some shredded coconut
5. Serve immediately.

Per Serving:
(Calories 350 | Total Fats 31.3g | Net Carbs: 4.2g | Protein 12.1g | Fiber: 3g)

Cheesy Eggs de Provence

(TotalTime: 30 MIN | Serves: 3)

Ingredients:

- 3 large eggs
- ½ small onion, finely chopped
- ½ cup bacon slices
- ¼ cup heavy cream
- ½ cup fresh kale, chopped
- ½ cup cheddar cheese

Spices:
- 1 tsp Herbs de Provence
- ¼ tsp sea salt
- ¼ tsp black pepper, ground

Directions:

1. In a large mixing bowl, combine eggs and heavy cream. With a paddle attachment, beat on high speed for 2 minutes or until light and fluffy mixture. Now, add bacon, kale, and cheddar cheese. Season with salt, pepper, and Herbs de Provence. Mix well again and transfer the mixture to the oven-safe baking dish.
2. Plug in your instant pot and pour 1 cup of water in the stainless steel insert. Set the trivet and place the baking dish on top.
3. Securely lock the lid and adjust the steam release handle. Press the "Manual" button and set the timer for 20 minutes. Cook on "High" pressure.
4. When done, release the pressure naturally and open the lid.
5. Carefully remove the dish from the pot and chill for a while before serving.

Per Serving:
(Calories 205 | Total Fats 16.1g | Net Carbs: 0.9g | Protein 12.5g | Fiber: 0.4g)

Breakfast Recipes

Vichyssoise

(TotalTime: 50 MIN| Serves: 4)

Ingredients:

For soup:
- 2 cups cauliflower, chopped
- 1 large leek, chopped
- 1 small onion, finely chopped
- 1 cup cream cheese
- 5 cups vegetable stock
- 3 tbsp butter
- 1 tsp lemon juice, freshly squeezed

Spices:
- 1/8 tsp nutmeg
- ¼ tsp dried parsley
- 1 bay leaf
- ½ tsp salt
- ¼ tsp white pepper, freshly ground
- Freshly snipped chives, optional

Directions:

1. Plug in your instant pot and press the "Sauté" button. Melt the butter in the stainless steel insert and add the leeks and onions. Stir-fry for about 4-5 minutes without browning.
2. Add the cauliflower, vegetable stock, lemon juice, nutmeg, parsley, and bay leaf. Sprinkle with salt and pepper and securely lock the lid. Press the "Manual" button and set the timer for 10 minutes. Cook on high pressure.
3. When done, press the "Cancel" button and move the pressure valve to the "Venting" position to release the pressure. Remove and discard the bay leaf and pour the soup through a large sieve. Alternatively, transfer to a food processor and process until smooth.
4. Pour the soup back to the pot and press the "Sauté" button. Stir in the cream cheese and optionally sprinkle with some more salt or pepper to taste. Cook for another 5 minutes, stirring constantly.
5. Press the "Cancel" button to turn off the pot. Transfer the soup to serving bowls and sprinkle with chives.
6. Serve immediately.

Per Serving:
(Calories 320| Total Fats 29.1g | Net Carbs: 7.4g | Protein: 6.5g |Fiber: 2.7g)

Spring Vegetable Stew

(TotalTime: 40 MIN| Serves: 6)

Ingredients:

For stew:
- 2 lbs beef stew meat
- 1 spring onion, chopped
- 2 large tomatoes, chopped
- 1 red bell pepper, finely chopped
- 1 cup zucchini, chopped
- 1 cup broccoli, chopped
- 1 cup spinach, chopped
- ¼ cup fresh parsley leaves
- 2 celery stalks, chopped
- 5 cups beef broth
- 4 tbsp butter
- 4 tbsp olive oil

Spices:
- 1 tsp sea salt
- ½ tsp dried rosemary
- ¼ tsp stevia powder
- 1 tsp smoked paprika
- 1 tbsp cayenne pepper
- ½ tsp onion powder

Directions:

1. Plug in the instant pot and grease the inner pot with olive oil. Press the "Sauté" button and heat up. Add spring onions and tomatoes. Season with some salt and cook for 4-5 minutes stirring constantly.
2. Press the "Cancel" button to turn off the heat. Now add bell broccoli, zucchini, celery stalks, bell peppers, spinach, and parsley, creating layers as you go. Pour in the broth and sprinkle with the remaining spices. Top with beef stew meat.
3. Seal the lid and set the steam release handle to the "Sealing" position. Press the "Meat" button.
4. When done, release the pressure naturally and open the lid. Mix all well and stir in the butter.
5. Serve immediately.

Per Serving:
(Calories 490| Total Fats 27.9g | Net Carbs: 5g | Protein: 51.7g |Fiber: 2g)

Breakfast Recipes

Cottage Cheese Quiche

(TotalTime: 45 MIN | Serves: 4)

Ingredients:

- 8 large eggs
- ½ cup milk
- ½ cup almond flour
- 1 large red bell pepper, chopped
- 1 cup tomatoes, chopped
- 2 green onions, chopped
- 1 ½ cup cottage cheese

Spices:
- ¼ tsp salt
- ¼ tsp black pepper
- ½ tsp oregano

Directions:

1. Plug in your Instant Pot and place the trivet at the bottom of the stainless steel insert. Add aluminum foil over the trivet creating sling and pour in 1 cup of water. Set aside.
2. In a large mixing bowl, combine flour, salt, and black pepper. Optionally add some herbs of choice. Mix until completely incorporated. Gradually add eggs, one at the time beating constantly with a paddle mixing attachment. Pour in the milk and continue to beat for 2 minutes on medium speed.
3. Finally add vegetables and shredded vegan cheese. Mix again and transfer the mixture to oven-safe dish.
4. Gently place the dish in your Instant Pot and seal the lid. Set the steam release handle to the "Sealing" position and select the MANUAL mode. Set the timer for 30 minutes on HIGH pressure.
5. When done, release the pressure naturally for 10 minutes and move the pressure valve to the VENTING position to release any remaining steam.
6. Carefully open the lid and remove the dish using an aluminum sling. Chill for a while and serve.

Per Serving:
(Calories 276 | Total Fats 14g | Net Carbs: 9.2g | Protein 26.8g | Fiber: 1.5g)

Breakfast Recipes

Bacon and Cheese Egg Bake

(Total Time: 15 MIN | Serves: 4)

Ingredients:

- 8 eggs
- ½ cup milk
- 1 cup mozzarella cheese, shredded
- 8 pieces of bacon, chopped
- 2 cups cauliflower, chopped
- ¼ cup green onions, chopped

Spices:
- ½ tsp salt

Directions:

1. Plug in the instant pot and grease the inner pot with oil. Press the "Sauté" button and heat up.
2. Add chopped bacon and briefly cook for a couple of minutes or until lightly brown on all sides.
3. Using a wooden spatula spread the bacon evenly over the bottom of the pot creating the first layer.
4. Add chopped cauliflower creating the second layer in your pot. Set aside.
5. In another bowl, crack the eggs and season with salt. Pour in the milk and whisk together until foamy. Pour the mixture over cauliflower and top with mozzarella cheese.
6. Seal the lid and press the "Manual" button. Set the timer for 7 minutes on high pressure.
7. When done, perform a quick pressure release and open the lid. Sprinkle with green onions and serve immediately.

Per Serving:
(Calories 381g | Total Fats 26.6g | Net Carbs: 4.7g | Protein 29.3g | Fiber: 1.4g)

Chapter 3
Curries and Indian Inspired Dishes

Chicken Biryani

(TotalTime: 55 MIN | Serves: 4)

Ingredients:

For eggs:
- 1 lb chicken thighs, skin-on
- 2 cups cauliflower, chopped into florets
- 2 small onions, finely chopped
- 2 cups chicken stock
- 1 ½ cup heavy cream
- 2 tbsp apple cider vinegar
- 3 tbsp ghee

Spices:
- 1 tsp cloves
- ½ tsp chili powder
- ¼ tsp chili flakes
- 2 tsp turmeric powder
- 1 tsp ground mace
- 2 tsp coriander powder
- 2 cinnamon sticks
- 2 bay leaves
- 1 tbsp cloves

Directions:

1. In a medium-sized bowl, combine together heavy cream, apple cider, and spices. Whisk together and add chicken drumsticks. Coat well with the marinade and transfer to large Ziploc bag. Seal the bag and refrigerate overnight.
2. Grease a small baking dish with ghee and add cauliflower. Remove the chicken from the refrigerator and place in the bowl along with spices. Stir well and tightly wrap with aluminum foil.
3. Plug in the instant pot and set the trivet at the bottom of inner pot. Pour in 2 cups of water and place the pan on top.
4. Seal the lid and set the steam release handle to the "Sealing" position. Press the "Manual" button and set the timer for 25 minutes on high pressure.
5. When done, perform a quick release and open the lid. Serve immediately.

Per Serving:
(Calories 444 | Total Fats 30g | Net Carbs: 5.6g | Protein: 35.5g | Fiber: 2g)

Curries and Indian Inspired Dishes

Cauliflower Lamb Curry

(Total Time: 45 MIN | Serves: 4)

Ingredients:

- 1 lb lamb stew meat, cubed
- 2 cups cauliflower florets
- 1 cup zucchini chunks
- 4 garlic cloves, minced
- 1 cup coconut milk, full-fat
- 2 tbsp apple cider vinegar
- 3 tbsp ghee

Spices:
- 2 tbsp garam masala
- ¼ cup chopped cilantro
- 2 tbsp fresh ginger, grated
- 2 tsp turmeric powder
- 1 tsp black pepper, freshly ground

Directions:

1. Rinse the meat and place in a bowl with a tight lid. Season with garlic, ginger, salt, and pepper. Pour in the coconut milk and apple cider. Mix well and seal the lid. Refrigerate for 30 minutes.
2. Remove the meat from the refrigerator and place in the pot along with the cauliflower, ghee, garam masala, and turmeric powder.
3. Stir well and seal the lid. Set the steam release handle to the "Sealing" position and press the "Manual" button.
4. Set the timer for 20 minutes on high pressure. When done, release the pressure by moving the pressure valve to the "Venting" position.
5. Open the lid and stir in zucchini. Seal the lid again and continue to cook for another 5 minutes on the "Manual" mode.
6. When done, perform a quick release and open the lid.
7. Stir in cilantro and serve immediately.

Per Serving:
(Calories 457| Total Fats 32.3g | Net Carbs: 5.1g | Protein: 34.8g |Fiber: 3g)

Ginger Pork

(TotalTime: 60 MIN | Serves: 3)

Ingredients:

- 2 lbs pork loin, chopped into bite-sized pieces
- 1 cup eggplant, chopped
- 3 tbsp ghee
- 1 spring onion, finely chopped
- 3 garlic cloves
- 3 cups beef stock
- 2 tbsp light soy sauce
- 1 tbsp anka sauce
- 1 tbsp balsamic vinegar

Spices:
- 2 tsp ginger powder
- 1 anise star
- 3 cloves
- 2 tsp sea salt

Directions:

1. Place the meat at the bottom of the instant pot and pour in enough water to cover. Press the "Sauté" button and gently bring it to a boil. Cook for 5 minutes, stirring occasionally. Remove from the pot and drain. Set aside.
2. Now grease the inner pot with ghee and heat up. Add spring onions, ginger powder, anise, and cloves. Simmer for 1 minute, stirring constantly.
3. Pour in the anka sauce and continue to cook for another minute. Add the meat and mix well.
4. Finally, add the remaining ingredients and seal the lid. Set the steam release handle and press the "Manual" button. Set the timer for 35 minutes on high pressure.
5. When done, perform a quick pressure release and open the lid.
6. Serve immediately.

Per Serving:
(Calories 576 | Total Fats 24g | Net Carbs: 2.9g | Protein: 82.7g | Fiber: 1.2g)

Curries and Indian Inspired Dishes

Spicy Lamb

(Total Time: 45 MIN | Serves: 6)

Ingredients:

- 2 lbs boneless leg of lamb, cut into bite-sized pieces
- ¼ cup heavy cream
- 2 tbsp ghee
- 2 cups cherry tomatoes, chopped
- 3 cups vegetable stock

Spices:
- 1 tsp salt
- 1 tbsp coriander powder
- 1 tsp ginger powder
- 1 tsp cumin powder
- 2 tbsp chili powder
- 1 tsp garam masala
- ½ tsp garlic powder
- 2 tsp fennel seeds
- 1 ½ tsp cumin seeds
- 3 cloves, whole
- 1 cinnamon stick
- 3 bay leaves

Directions:

1. Rinse the meat under cold running water and pat dry with a kitchen paper. Place on a clean work surface and chop into bite-sized pieces. Place in a deep bowl and add heavy cream and garam masala. Stir well and tightly wrap with aluminum foil. Refrigerate overnight.
2. Plug in the instant pot and press the "Sauté" button. Grease the inner pot with ghee and add bay leaves, cardamom, cinnamon, cloves, cumin seeds, and fennel seeds. Briefly cook for 1-2 minutes, stirring constantly with a wooden spatula.
3. Now add the remaining spices and stir well again. Continue to cook for another minute.
4. Finally, add the meat along with the heavy cream. Pour in the stock and add cherry tomatoes. Stir well and seal the lid. Set the steam release handle and press the "Manual" button.
5. Set the timer for 25 minutes on high pressure.
6. When done, release the pressure naturally and open the lid. Stir well again and serve immediately.

Per Serving:
(Calories 350 | Total Fats 17.4g | Net Carbs: 1.9g | Protein: 43.3g | Fiber: 1g)

Curries and Indian Inspired Dishes

Eggplant Curry

(TotalTime: 50 MIN | Serves: 4)

Ingredients:

- 2 lamb shanks
- 2 green chili peppers, whole
- 4 garlic cloves, whole
- 4 tbsp ghee
- 4 cups beef broth
- 4 tbsp yogurt
- ½ eggplant, cubed

Spices:
- 1 tbsp smoked paprika
- 1 tbsp oregano
- 2 tsp salt
- 2 tbsp cumin seeds
- 2 cinnamon sticks
- 2 bay leaves

Directions:

1. Place the meat in a large bowl. Generously sprinkle with salt, pepper, garlic, paprika, oregano, and cumin seeds.
2. Plug in the instant pot and press the "Sauté" button. Grease the inner pot with ghee and add the meat. Cook for 3-4 minutes, stirring constantly.
3. When the meat is nicely browned on all sides, sprinkle with some more spices and add eggplants. Cook for 5 minutes.
4. Pour in the broth and add yogurt and chili peppers. Stir well and seal the lid. Set the steam release handle to the "Sealing" position and press the "Manual" button.
5. Set the timer for 30 minutes on high pressure.
6. When done, release the pressure naturally and open the lid. Chill for a while and serve.

Per Serving:
(Calories 392 | Total Fats 22.7g | Net Carbs: 4.3g | Protein: 38.4g | Fiber: 2.2g)

Classic Ginger Curry

(TotalTime: 35 MIN | Serves: 6)

Ingredients:

- 2 lbs leg of lamb, chopped into bite-sized pieces
- 1 onion, finely chopped
- 3 garlic cloves, minced
- 5 chili peppers, whole
- 2 cups tomatoes, chopped
- 3 tbsp ghee
- 4 cups vegetable broth

Spices:
- 3 tbsp fresh ginger, grated
- 2 tsp fennel powder
- 1 tsp cumin powder
- ½ tsp cinnamon powder
- ½ black pepper, freshly ground
- 5 cloves
- ½ tsp coriander powder
- ½ tsp nutmeg powder
- 2 tsp turmeric powder
- 2 tbsp cayenne pepper
- 2 tsp salt
- 1 tsp cardamom powder

Directions:

1. Plug in the instant pot and press the "Sauté" button. Grease the inner pot with ghee and add the meat. Cook for 4-5 minutes or until lightly browned. Remove from the pot and transfer to a large platter.
2. Now add onions, garlic, chilies, and ginger. Continue to cook for another 3-4 minutes, or until the onions are translucent and chilies soft. Stir well and add tomatoes.
3. Cook for 3-4 minutes, stirring constantly and then sprinkle with the remaining spices. Pour in the broth and give it a good stir.
4. Seal the lid and set the steam release handle to the "Sealing" position. Press the "Stew" button.
5. When done, release the pressure naturally and open the lid. Give it a good stir again and serve immediately.

Per Serving:
(Calories 385| Total Fats 18.5g | Net Carbs: 4.1g | Protein: 46.6g |Fiber: 1.3g)

Tomato Rasam

(Total Time: 60 MIN | Serves: 5)

Ingredients:

- 1 lb beef stew meat
- 2 large tomatoes, chopped
- 2 red chilies, finely chopped
- 1 small onion, finely chopped
- 4 tbsp ghee
- 2 garlic cloves, crushed
- 5 cups vegetable stock

Spices:
- 2 tsp salt
- 2 tsp stevia powder
- 2 tsp turmeric powder
- 2 tsp hing
- 2 tsp mustard seeds
- 2 tsp coriander powder
- 2 tbsp chili powder

Directions:

1. Plug in the instant pot and pour in the stock. Add tomatoes, onions, and chili peppers. Stir well and press the "Sauté" button. Bring it to a boil and gently simmer for 15 minutes.
2. Now stir in the meat and season with all spices. Add the remaining ingredients and stir well.
3. Seal the lid and set the steam release handle to the "Sealing" position. Press the "Manual" button and set the timer for 40 minutes on high pressure.
4. When done, release the pressure naturally and open the lid. Stir well again and serve immediately.

Per Serving:
(Calories 285 | Total Fats 16.1g | Net Carbs: 5.6g | Protein: 28.8g | Fiber: 1.8g)

Keto Sambar

(TotalTime: 55 MIN | Serves: 6)

Ingredients:

- 2 lbs pork chops, cut into bite-sized pieces
- 2 small tomatoes, chopped
- 2 cups cauliflower, chopped into florets
- 1 cup eggplant, chopped into chunks
- 1 large onion, finely chopped
- 2 chili peppers, whole
- 3 garlic cloves, crushed
- 4 tbsp ghee
- 4 cups vegetable stock
- 1 cup coconut milk

Spices:
- 2 tsp sambar powder
- 1 tbsp jiggery powder
- 2 tsp salt
- 1 tsp black pepper
- ¼ cup fresh parsley, finely chopped
- 3 tsp turmeric powder
- 2 tbsp chili powder
- 3 tbsp brown mustard seeds

Directions:

1. Place vegetables in a large colander and rinse well. Drain and set aside.
2. Cut the meat into bite-sized pieces. Place in a deep bowl and sprinkle with salt and pepper. Set aside.
3. Plug in the instant pot and grease the inner pot with ghee. Press the "Sauté" button and add mustard seeds. Cook for 1 minute and then add onions, garlic, and chili pepper. Stir well and cook for 3-4 minutes.
4. Now add cauliflower and eggplant. Pour in some of the stock and bring it to a boil. Simmer for 5 minutes.
5. Finally, add the remaining ingredients and stir well. Seal the lid and set the steam release handle to the "Sealing" position and press the "Manual" button.
6. Set the timer for 35 minutes on high pressure.
7. When done, release the pressure naturally and optionally sprinkle with some more fresh parsley.
8. Serve immediately.

Per Serving:
(Calories 600 | Total Fats 46.3g | Net Carbs: 4.8g | Protein: 36.1g | Fiber: 3.8g)

Curries and Indian Inspired Dishes

Rajma Masala with Cauliflower

(TotalTime: 25 MIN| Serves: 4)

Ingredients:

- 1 lb cauliflower, cut into florets
- 1 cup cherry tomatoes, chopped
- 1 small onion, finely chopped
- 3 chili peppers, chopped
- 4 tbsp ghee
- 3 tbsp oil
- 3 cups vegetable stock

Spices:
- 2 tbsp coriander seeds
- 1 tsp salt
- 2 tbsp chili powder
- 3 tsp garam masala
- 1 tbsp fresh ginger, grated
- ¼ cup fresh parsley, finely chopped

Directions:

1. Grease the inner pot with oil and add coriander seeds and chili peppers. Cook for 3-4 minutes, stirring constantly.
2. Now add onions and season with all spices. Stir well and continue to cook for another 3-4 minutes.
3. Add the remaining ingredients and pour in the stock. Stir well and seal the lid. Set the steam release handle to the "Sealing" position and press the "Manual" button.
4. Set the timer for 15 minutes on high pressure.
5. When done, release the pressure naturally and open the lid. Serve immediately.

Per Serving:

(Calories 251| Total Fats 23.3g | Net Carbs: 6g | Protein: 3.2g |Fiber: 4.3g)

Curries and Indian Inspired Dishes

Keto Pav Bhaji

(TotalTime: 45 MIN| Serves: 4)

Ingredients:

- 2 cups cauliflower, chopped into florets
- 1 small bell pepper, finely chopped
- 1 cup cherry tomatoes
- 1 large onion, finely chopped
- 4 tbsp butter, softened
- 2 cups vegetable stock

Spices:
- 3 tsp garam masala
- 2 tbsp cumin seeds
- 2 tbsp mustard seeds
- 1 tbsp chili powder
- 1 tsp salt
- 3 tsp turmeric powder
- ¼ cup fresh parsley, finely chopped

For the pav:
- 3 slices of your favorite keto bread
- 3 tbsp butter
- 1 tsp salt

Directions:

1. Plug in the instant pot and press the "Sauté" button. Add cauliflower and vegetable stock. Stir well and cook for 15 minutes or until fork-tender.
2. Remove from the pot and transfer to a deep bowl. Reserve the liquid in the pot.
3. Using a potato masher, mash cauliflower until smooth and place back to the pot. add the remaining ingredients and stir well. Season with spices and seal the lid.
4. Set the steam release handle to the "Sealing" position and press the "Manual" button.
5. Set the timer for 13 minutes on high pressure.
6. When done, release the pressure naturally and carefully open the lid. Press the "Sauté" button again and cook until most of the liquid evaporates. Stir well and remove from the pot.
7. To prepare the keto pav, keep the instant pot on the "Sauté" mode and melt butter. Sprinkle with salt and add bread slices. Fry for 2-3 minutes on each side.
8. Remove from the pot and serve with bhaji.

Per Serving:
(Calories 226| Total Fats 20.5g | Net Carbs: 7.4g | Protein: 2.5g |Fiber: 3.2g)

Curries and Indian Inspired Dishes

Paneer Butter Masala

(TotalTime: 25 MIN | Serves: 4)

Ingredients:

- 2 cups cherry tomatoes, chopped
- 2 red chili peppers, chopped
- 5 garlic cloves, crushed
- 1 cup cottage cheese
- 5 tbsp butter, softened
- 1 cup vegetable stock

Spices:
- 1 tbsp chili powder
- 1 tbsp coriander seeds
- ½ tbsp. garam masala powder
- 1 tsp ginger powder
- 1 cinnamon stick
- ½ tsp salt

Directions:

1. Plug in the instant pot and press the "Sauté" button. Add butter and heat up.
2. Add chili peppers and cook for 2-3 minutes, stirring once. Then add garlic and continue to cook for another minute.
3. Now add tomatoes and pour in half of the stock. Simmer for 5 minutes and then add the remaining spices.
4. Pour in the remaining broth and seal the lid. Set the steam release handle to the "Sealing" position and press the "Manual" button. Set timer for 5 minutes on high pressure.
5. When done, perform a quick pressure release by moving the pressure valve to the "Venting" position and carefully open the lid.
6. Chill masala to a room temperature and transfer to a food processor. Process until smooth and divide between serving bowls.
7. Stir in cottage cheese in each bowl and serve.

Per Serving:
(Calories 202 | Total Fats 15.7g | Net Carbs: 5.8g | Protein: 9.1g | Fiber: 1.4g)

Chicken Curry

(TotalTime: 60 MIN | Serves: 5)

Ingredients:

- 2 lbs chicken wings
- 4 tbsp butter (can be replaced with ghee)
- 1 large onion, finely chopped
- 1 large tomato, roughly chopped
- 2 garlic cloves, crushed
- 1 cup cauliflower, chopped into florets
- 5 cups chicken stock

Spices:
- 4 tbsp fresh parsley, finely chopped
- 2 tsp garam masala
- 2 tsp salt
- 1 tbsp cayenne pepper
- 2 tsp turmeric powder
- 1 tsp white pepper, freshly ground
- 2 tbsp coriander powder
- 2 tsp ginger powder

Directions:

1. Grease the inner pot with butter and press the "Sauté" button. Heat up and add onions and garlic. Stir-fry for 3-4 minutes and then add tomato. Continue to cook until tomato has completely softened.
2. Add chicken wings and season with spices. Cook for another 5 minutes, turning the wings several times.
3. Finally, pour in the stock and add the remaining ingredients. Seal the lid and set the steam release handle.
4. Press the "Manual" button and set the timer for 40 minutes on high pressure.
5. When done, release the pressure naturally and open the lid. Stir well again and serve.

Per Serving:
(Calories 391 | Total Fats 15.4g | Net Carbs: 4.8g | Protein: 54.5g | Fiber: 1.6g)

Chili Tomato Stew

(TotalTime: 40 MIN | Serves: 6)

Ingredients:

- 1 lb chicken breast, chopped into bite-sized pieces
- 2 cups fire-roasted tomatoes, diced
- 2 cups coconut milk
- 2 cups chicken stock
- 3 celery stalks, chopped
- 3 red chili peppers, finely chopped
- 1 small onion, finely chopped
- 3 garlic cloves, crushed
- 2 cups button mushrooms, sliced
- 5 tbsp ghee

Spices:
- 2 tbsp chili powder
- 1 tbsp garam masala
- 2 tsp turmeric powder
- 1 tbsp mustard seeds
- 4 cloves
- ½ tsp ginger powder

Directions:

1. Plug in the instant pot and press the "Sauté" button. Melt the ghee in the inner pot and add celery, onions, and garlic. Sprinkle with turmeric powder and stir well. Cook for 4-5 minutes.
2. Now add chili peppers and ginger powder. Continue to cook for another 3-4 minutes.
3. Finally, add mushrooms and season with the remaining spices. Cook until all the liquid evaporates.
4. Add the remaining ingredients and seal the lid. Set the steam release handle to the "Sealing" position and press the "Meat" button.
5. When done, release the pressure naturally and open the lid. Stir well again and serve immediately.

Per Serving:
(Calories 389 | Total Fats 31.9g | Net Carbs: 6g | Protein: 19.5g | Fiber: 3.1g)

Curries and Indian Inspired Dishes

Coconut Turkey Curry

(TotalTime: 45 MIN| Serves: 5)

Ingredients:

- 1 lb turkey breast, chopped into bite-sized pieces
- 1 medium-sized onion, finely chopped
- 1 cup broccoli, chopped
- 2 cups coconut milk
- 3 cups chicken stock
- 3 tbsp ghee

Spices:
- 1 tsp salt
- 1 tsp black pepper, freshly ground
- 2 tsp garlic powder
- 2 tbsp curry powder
- 1 tbsp chili powder

Directions:

1. Plug in the instant pot and add onions in the inner pot. Press the "Sauté" button and cook for 3-4 minutes, or until translucent.
2. Now add broccoli and season with spices. Stir well and continue to cook for 5 minutes.
3. Pour in the coconut milk and chicken stock. Add ghee and seal the lid.
4. Set the steam release handle and press the "Manual" button. Set the timer for 20 minutes on high pressure.
5. When done, perform a quick release by moving the pressure valve to the "Venting" position.
6. Carefully open the lid and serve immediately.

Per Serving:
(Calories 403 | Total Fats: 32.5g | Net Carbs: 9.3g | Protein: 18.9g |Fiber: 3.5g)

Butter Lamb Shoulder

(TotalTime: 50 MIN | Serves: 5)

Ingredients:

- 2 lbs lamb shoulder, chopped
- 3 tbsp butter
- 2 cups beef broth
- ½ eggplant, cubed
- 4 garlic cloves, crushed
- 1 tomato, chopped

Spices:
- 1 ½ tsp salt
- 1 tsp black pepper, ground
- 2 tsp cumin powder
- 2 tsp coriander powder
- 1 tsp onion powder
- 1 tbsp ginger, freshly grated
- 1 cinnamon stick

Directions:

1. In a small bowl, combine salt, black pepper, cumin powder, coriander powder, and grated ginger. Set aside.
2. Rinse well the meat and rub with spices. Set aside.
3. Plug in the instant pot and press the "Sauté" button. Grease the inner pot with butter and heat up. Add meat, in several batches, and cook for 4-5 minutes, turning once. Remove from the pot and set aside.
4. Now add eggplant and garlic. Season with some salt and cook for 5 minutes, stirring constantly. Add tomatoes and give it a good stir. Continue to cook for another minute.
5. Now add the meat and pour in the broth. Seal the lid.
6. Set the steam release handle to the "Sealing" position and press the "Manual" button. Cook for 25 minutes on high pressure.
7. When done, release the pressure naturally and open the lid. Serve immediately.
8. Optionally, use the "Slow Cooker" mode and cook for 8 hours on low.

Per Serving:
(Calories 431 | Total Fats: 20.9g | Net Carbs: 2.5g | Protein: 53.7g | Fiber: 1.8g)

Curries and Indian Inspired Dishes

Saffron Cauliflower Rice with Pork

(Total Time: 60 MIN | Serves: 4)

Ingredients:

- 1 lb pork leg roast, boneless and cut into bite-sized pieces
- 2 cups cauliflower florets
- ¼ cup apple cider vinegar
- 3 garlic cloves
- 3 tbsp oil
- 4 tbsp ghee
- 2 cups vegetable stock
- 2 tbsp sesame seeds
- 2 small onions, finely chopped

Spices:
- 1 tsp cinnamon powder
- 1 tsp turmeric powder
- 2 cardamom pods, bruised
- 1 ½ tsp salt
- 1 tsp black pepper, freshly ground
- 2 bay leaves
- 1 cinnamon stick
- 1 tsp cumin powder
- ½ tsp ginger powder
- 2 tsp turmeric power
- 2 tsp saffron threads

Directions:

1. Whisk together oil, turmeric powder, ginger powder, and cinnamon powder until a smooth paste. Set aside.
2. Rinse the meat and pat dry with a kitchen towel. Place on a large cutting board and chop into bite-sized pieces. Lightly brush each piece with the oil mixture and set aside.
3. Plug the instant pot and press the "Sauté" button. Grease the inner pot with ghee and heat up. Add onions and cook until translucent, stirring constantly with a wooden spatula. Remove from the pot and set aside.
4. Now add the meat and brown for 7-8 minutes, stirring occasionally.
5. Pour in the stock and add onions along with the remaining ingredients. Seal the lid and cook for 20 minutes on the "Manual" mode.
6. When done, perform a quick pressure release and open the lid.
7. Preheat the oven to 450 degrees. Transfer the mixture to a greased baking dish and bake for 15 minutes.
8. Remove from the oven and chill for a while. Sprinkle with saffron and serve.

Per Serving:
(Calories 426 | Total Fats: 29.3g | Net Carbs: 5.5g | Protein: 32.2g | Fiber: 2.8g)

Curries and Indian Inspired Dishes

Turmeric Chicken

(TotalTime: 40 MIN | Serves: 4)

Ingredients:

- 2 pieces of chicken breast, about 1 lb
- 1 large onion, finely chopped
- 4 garlic cloves, whole
- 1 cup beef broth
- 1 cup cherry tomatoes
- ¼ cup almonds, raw
- ¼ cup Greek yogurt
- 3 tbsp ghee

Spices:
- 2 tsp turmeric powder
- 5 cloves, whole
- ½ tsp ginger powder
- 3 tsp chili powder
- ¼ cup coriander, finely chopped

Directions:

1. Plug in the instant pot and press the "Sauté" button. Melt the ghee and add onions and garlic. Stir well and cook for 3-4 minutes. Now add cherry tomatoes and cloves. Continue to cook for another 5 minutes.
2. Meanwhile, rinse the meat and chop into bite-sized pieces. Sprinkle with turmeric and add to the pot.
3. Briefly brows, stirring constantly and season with the remaining spices. Cook for one minute. Remove from the pot and add almonds. Cook until lightly toasted. If necessary, add some more ghee.
4. Place the chicken back to the pot and give it a good stir. Pour in the broth and seal the lid.
5. Set the steam release handle to the "Sealing" position and press the "Manual" button.
6. Set the timer for 15 minutes on high pressure.
7. When done, perform a quick pressure release and open the lid. Remove the chicken from the pot and chill for a while.
8. Top with Greek yogurt and serve.

Per Serving:
(Calories 336| Total Fats: 16.7g | Net Carbs: 6.1g | Protein: 37.6g | Fiber: 2.1g)

Simple Palak Paneer

(Total Time: 15 MIN | Serves: 4)

Ingredients:

- 1 cup feta cheese, cubed
- 3 cups fresh spinach, chopped
- ¼ cup cashews
- 3 garlic cloves, minced
- 1 small green chili pepper, seeds removed and chopped
- 1 small onion, chopped
- 1 cup tomatoes, diced
- 2 tbsp butter

Spices:
- 2 tsp fresh ginger, grated
- 1 cardamom pod
- ¼ tsp garam masala powder
- ½ tsp salt
- ½ tsp coriander powder
- ¼ tsp black pepper, ground

Directions:

1. Using a large colander, rinse the spinach under running water. Drain and torn into small pieces. Transfer to a food processor along with cashews, chili pepper, garlic, and grated ginger. Add 2 tbsp of water and blend until smooth and creamy.
2. Plug in your instant pot and press the "Saute" button. Melt the butter in the stainless steel insert and add onions. Sprinkle with salt, garam masala, cardamom, and coriander powder. Cook for 3-4 minutes and then add tomatoes and spinach mixture. Securely lock the lid and press the "Manual" button. Set the timer for 2 minutes and cook on "High" pressure.
3. When you hear the cooker's end signal, perform a quick release of the pressure by moving the valve to the "Venting" position.
4. Open the pot and stir in the cubed feta cheese.
5. Transfer to a serving pot and serve immediately.

Per Serving:
(Calories 227 | Total Fats 18g | Net Carbs: 8.2g | Protein: 8.2g | Fiber: 1.9g)

Indian Broccoli Shrimp

(Total Time: 20 MIN | Serves: 3)

Ingredients:

- 1 lb jumbo shrimps, frozen
- 1 medium-sized tomato, diced
- 1 cup broccoli, chopped
- 2 tbsp coconut oil
- 2 medium-sized red onions, chopped
- 1 tbsp almonds, chopped
- 2 cups fish stock

Spices:
- ½ tsp cumin seeds
- 1 tsp smoked paprika, ground
- 1 whole clove
- 2 cardamom pods
- ½ tsp garam masala powder
- 1 tsp salt
- ¼ tsp garlic powder
- ¼ tsp ginger powder
- 4-5 curry leaves

Directions:

1. Plug in your instant pot and grease the stainless steel insert with coconut oil. Press the "Saute" button and add almonds. Cook for 2-3 minutes, stirring constantly. Remove from the pot and set aside.
2. Now, add onions, cumin seeds, clove, and cardamom pods. Stir-fry for 3-4 minutes, or until onions translucent.
3. Add smoked paprika, garam masala, salt, garlic powder, ginger powder, and curry leaves. Cook for a minute and then add shrimps., broccoli, and tomato.
4. Pour in the fish stock and stir well. Securely lock the lid and press the "Manual" button. Set the timer for 8 minutes and cook on "High" pressure.
5. When you hear the cooker's end signal, release the pressure naturally.
6. Open the pot and stir in the almonds.
7. Serve immediately.

Per Serving:
(Calories 284 | Total Fats 12.1g | Net Carbs: 9.1g | Protein: 33.4g | Fiber: 4.3g)

Spicy Lamb Coriander Curry

(TotalTime: 60 MIN | Serves: 4)

Ingredients:

- 2 lbs leg of lamb
- 4 garlic cloves, finely chopped
- 1 medium-sized onion
- 1 medium-sized red bell pepper
- 1 cup tomatoes, diced
- 2 cups beef stock
- ½ cup fresh coriander, chopped
- 1 tbsp olive oil

Spices:
- 1 tsp garam masala powder
- 2 tsp fresh ginger, grated
- 1 tsp fennel seeds
- 1 tsp red chili powder
- 1 tsp cumin seeds
- 1 tsp salt
- ½ tsp black pepper, ground

Directions:

1. Plug in your instant pot and grease the stainless steel insert with olive oil. Press the "Saute" button and add onions, cumin seeds, and fennel seeds. Cook for 3-4 minutes, or until the onions translucent.
2. Add bell pepper and tomatoes. Stir well and bring it to a ligh simmer. Sprinkle with garam masala, ginger, and red chili powder.
3. Finally, add meat and pour in the beef stock. Stir in the coriander and close the lid.
4. Set the steam release handle and press the "Manual" button. Set the timer for 40 minutes and cook on "High" pressure.
5. When you hear the cookers end signal, perform a quick release of the pressure. Open the pot and press the "Saute" button. Cook for 10 more minutes, or until the liquid reduces to a desired consistency.
6. Optionally, sprinkle with some finely chopped cilantro before serving.

Per Serving:
(Calories 503 | Total Fats 21g | Net Carbs: 7g | Protein: 66.7g | Fiber: 2.3g)

Curries and Indian Inspired Dishes

Tandoori Chicken

(TotalTime: 20 MIN| Serves: 4)

Ingredients:

- 2 lbs chicken breasts, skinless and boneless
- 1 cup plain yogurt, full-fat
- 1 cup chicken broth
- 2 tbsp lime juice, freshly squeezed
- 2 garlic cloves, minced
- 1 tbsp olive oil

Spices:
- 1 tsp garam masala powder
- 1 tsp cumin seeds
- 2 tsp fresh ginger, grated
- 1 tsp onion powder
- 1 tsp coriander powder
- 1 tsp smoked paprika, ground
- 1 tsp salt

Directions:

1. Rinse the meat under cold running water and pat dry with a kitchen paper. Cut into thin slices and set aside.
2. In a large bowl, combine yogurt, lime juice, crushed garlic, and all spices. Mix until well combined and add chicken breasts. Coat well with marinade and refrigerate for 20 minutes.
3. Plug in your instant pot and press the "Saute" button. Melt the butter in th stainless steel insert and add chicken. Cook for 3 minutes on each side, or until lightly browned.
4. Now, pour in the broth and securely lock the lid.
5. Set the steam release handle and press the "Manual" button. Set the timer for 8 minutes and cook on "High" pressure.
6. When you hear the cooker's end signal, perform a quick releaese of the pressure by moving the valve to the "Venting" position.
7. Open the pot and transfer the chicken to a serving plate.
8. Optionally, serve with mashed cauliflower and sprinkle with some finely chopped green onions before serving.
9. Enjoy!

Per Serving:
(Calories 528 | Total Fats 21.7g | Net Carbs: 6.1g | Protein: 70.8g |Fiber: 0.5g)

Curries and Indian Inspired Dishes

Simple Chicken Vindaloo

 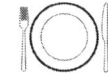

(TotalTime: 20 MIN | Serves: 4)

Ingredients:

- 3 lbs chicken thighs, skinless
- 3 small green chili peppers, chopped
- 2 medium-sized onions, chopped
- 4 garlic cloves, minced
- 2 tbsp butter
- 1 tbsp apple cider vinegar
- 1 cup chicken broth

Spices:
- 1 tsp mustard seeds
- ½ tsp cumin seeds
- ½ tsp coriander seeds
- ½ tsp turmeric powder
- 1 tsp salt
- 1 tsp black peppercorns, whole

Directions:

1. Plug in your instant pot and press the "Saute" button. Melt the butter in the stainless steel insert and add all spices. Fry for 3 minutes, stirring constantly.
2. Remove the seeds from the pot and transfer to a food processor. Add garlic and apple cider vinegar. Pulse until well combined. Coat the chicken thighs with this paste and set aside.
3. Now, add onions and green chili peppers to the pot. Cook for 3-4 minutes, or until the onions translucent. Add chicken thighs and cook for 2 minutes on each side.
4. Pour in the chicken broth and securely lock the lid.
5. Adjust the steam release handle and press the "Manual" button. Set the timer for 5 minutes and cook on "High" pressure.
6. When you hear the cooker's end signal, perform a quick release of the pressure and turn off the pot.
7. Transfer the chicken to a serving plate and serve immediately.

Per Serving:
(Calories 528 | Total Fats 21.7g | Net Carbs: 6.1g | Protein: 70.8g | Fiber: 0.5g)

Chapter 4

Seafood

Squid Rings with Potato and Spinach

(TotalTime: 35 MIN | Serves: 3)

Ingredients:

- 1 lb squid rings, frozen
- 1 lb fresh spinach, torn
- 2 cups cauliflower, roughly chopped
- 4 tbsp extra virgin olive oil
- 2 tbsp lemon juice

Spices:
- 1 tsp garlic paste
- 1 tsp dried rosemary, crushed
- 2 thyme sprigs, fresh
- 1 tsp sea salt

Directions:

1. Place squid rings in a deep bowl and pour in enough warm water to cover. Let it sit for a while. Transfer to a large colander and drain. Set aside.
2. Plug in the instant pot and grease the inner pot with two tablespoons of olive oil. Press the "Sauté" button and add garlic paste and rosemary. Stir-fry for one minute and then add the spinach. Season with salt and cook for 3-4 minutes or until wilted. Remove the spinach from the pot and set aside.
3. Add the remaining oil to the pot and heat up on the "Sauté" mode. Add chopped cauliflower making an even layer. Top with squid rings and drizzle with lemon juice and optionally some more olive oil to taste. Sprinkle with salt, add thyme sprigs, and pour in one cup of water (or fish stock).
4. Seal the lid and set the steam release handle to the "Sealing" position. Press the "Fish" button and set the timer for 9 minutes.
5. When you hear the cooker's end signal, carefully move the pressure valve to the "Venting" position to release the pressure.
6. Open the pot and stir in the spinach. Optionally, season with some more garlic powder or dried thyme.
7. Serve immediately.

Per Serving:
(Calories 353 | Total Fats 21.5g | Net Carbs: 8.9g | Protein: 29.3g | Fiber: 5g)

Seafood

Classic Fish Stew

(Total Time: 30 MIN | Serves: 6)

Ingredients:

- 2 lbs pollock fillets, skinless
- 1 lb king prawns, raw shelled
- ½ cup extra virgin olive oil
- 2 small onions, finely chopped
- 2 celery stalks, finely chopped
- 1 cup fresh parsley, finely chopped
- 3 garlic cloves, crushed
- 3 cups fish stock

Spices:
- 1 tsp sea salt
- 1 tbsp fresh rosemary, finely chopped

Directions:

1. Plug in the instant pot and grease the inner pot with three tablespoons of olive oil.
2. Add onions and crushed garlic. Press the "Sauté" button and cook for 4-5 minutes, stirring constantly.
3. Now, add the remaining ingredients and stir all well. Press the "Cancel" button to turn off the "Sauté" mode.
4. Seal the lid and set the steam release handle. Press the "Manual" button and set the timer for 10 minutes.
5. When done, press the "Cancel" button again and perform a quick pressure release by moving the pressure valve to the "Venting" position.
6. Carefully open the lid and sprinkle the stew with some freshly squeezed lemon juice before serving.

Per Serving:
(Calories 557 | Total Fats 32g | Net Carbs: 3.6g | Protein: 60.8g | Fiber: 1g)

Seafood

Orange Glazed Salmon Fillets

(Total Time: 20 MIN | Serves: 3)

Ingredients:

- 1 lb salmon fillets, about 1-inch thick
- 1 garlic clove, crushed
- 3 tbsp butter
- 3 tbsp olive oil

Spices:
- ½ liquid stevia
- 1 tsp chili flakes
- 1 tsp orange extract
- 1 tsp smoked salt
- ¼ tsp dried thyme

Directions:

1. Rinse well the fillets under cold running water and pat-dry with a kitchen towel. Set aside.
2. Plug in the instant pot and press the "Sauté" button. Grease the inner pot with butter and heat up. Add garlic and briefly cook for one minute, stirring constantly.
3. Now add fillets and brown for 2-3 minutes on each side. Press the "Cancel" button and remove the salmon from the pot.
4. In a small bowl, whisk together olive oil, stevia, chili flakes, orange extract, salt, and thyme. Brush fillets with this mixture and set aside.
5. Now set the steam basket in the inner pot and place the fillets in it. Pour in 2 cups of water in the pot and seal the lid.
6. Set the steam release handle to the "Sealing" position and press the "Manual" button. Set the timer for 12 minutes on high pressure.
7. When done, perform a quick release and open the lid. Transfer the fillets to serving plates and optionally drizzle with some more olive oil.

Per Serving:
(Calories 423 | Total Fats 34.9g | Net Carbs: 0.3g | Protein: 29.5g | Fiber: 0g)

Seafood

Black Cauliflower Pasta

(Total Time: 20 MIN | Serves: 3)

Ingredients:

- 1 lb frozen seafood mix, defrosted
- 2 cups cauliflower, chopped into florets
- ½ cup olive oil
- 4 garlic cloves, crushed
- 2 tbsp apple cider vinegar
- 1 tsbp squid ink
- ¼ cup Parmesan cheese

Spices:
- 1 tsp sea salt
- 1 tbsp fresh parsley, finely chopped
- 1 tsp fresh rosemary, finely chopped

Directions:

1. Plug in the instant pot and grease the inner pot with three tablespoons of olive oil.
2. Press the "Sauté" button and heat up. Add crushed garlic and stir-fry for one minute.
3. Now, add seafood mix, parsley, chopped rosemary, and sprinkle with salt. Give it a good stir and pour in the remaining olive oil along with ¼ cup of water.
4. Add chopped cauliflower and stir in the squid ink. Securely lock the lid. Set the steam release handle and press the "Manual" button.
5. Set the timer for 5 minutes on high pressure.
6. When done, release the pressure naturally for about 10 minutes and then move the pressure valve to the "Venting" position to release the remaining pressure.
7. Carefully open the lid and sprinkle with Parmesan cheese.
8. Serve warm.

Per Serving:
(Calories 476| Total Fats 37g | Net Carbs: 6.8g | Protein: 25.9g |Fiber: 1.8g)

Seafood

Wild Alaskan Salmon

(TotalTime: 25 MIN| Serves: 4)

Ingredients:

- 1 lb wild Alaskan salmon, defrosted
- 1 lb fresh asparagus, chopped into bite-sized pieces
- 4 tbsp olive oil
- 1 tsp rice vinegar
- 1 tbsp butter
- 3 garlic cloves, finely chopped
- 1 tbsp freshly squeezed lemon juice

Spices:
- 1 tsp smoked salt
- 1 tbsp fresh rosemary, finely chopped
- ¼ tsp white pepper, freshly ground

Directions:

1. Rinse the fillets and chop into bite-sized pieces. Place in a deep bowl and sprinkle with salt, white pepper, and rosemary. Optionally, add some garlic powder. Mix well and set aside.
2. Plug in the instant pot and add the olive oil in the stainless steel insert. Press the "Sauté" button and heat up. Add chopped salmon and cook for 5-6 minutes.
3. Now add garlic and drizzle with rice vinegar and lemon juice. Continue to cook for another 2-3 minutes.
4. Finally, add chopped asparagus and stir in the butter. Cook for 3 minutes more.
5. Press the "Cancel" button and serve immediately.

Per Serving:
(Calories 323| Total Fats 24.1g | Net Carbs: 2.7g | Protein: 24.7g |Fiber: 2.5g)

Sweet Rosemary Cod Fillet

 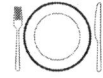

(TotalTime: 20 MIN| Serves: 6)

Ingredients:

- 2 lbs cod fillets, skinless
- ½ cup swerve
- ½ cup soy sauce
- 4 garlic cloves, crushed
- 4 tbsp butter
- 1 cup fish stock

Spices:
- 1 tsp sea salt
- ½ tsp white pepper, freshly ground
- 2 rosemary sprigs
- ¼ tsp dried rosemary

Directions:

1. Rub the fillets with salt, pepper, and dried rosemary. Place in the pot and add garlic, swerve, rosemary sprigs, and butter. Pour in the stock and drizzle with soy sauce. Press the "Sauté" button. Heat up and stir well to combine. Briefly cook for 2-3 minutes and press the "Cancel" button.
2. Seal the lid and set the steam release handle to the "Sealing" position. Press the "Manual" button and set the timer for 12 minutes.
3. When you hear the cooker's end signal, perform a quick pressure release and open the lid.
4. Now press the "Sauté" button again and gently simmer until half of the liquid evaporates and the sauce thickens.
5. Optionally, transfer the fillets along with the sauce in a small baking dish and bake for 10-15 minutes at 400 degrees F.

Per Serving:
(Calories 376| Total Fats 20.8g | Net Carbs: 2.3g | Protein: 42.7g |Fiber: 0.2g)

Seafood

Tomato Shrimp Stew

(TotalTime: 35 MIN | Serves: 4)

Ingredients:

- 1 lb shrimps, cleaned
- 2 large tomatoes, peeled and chopped
- 1 large onion, finely chopped
- 1 cup broccoli, chopped
- 1 cup collard greens, chopped
- 3 garlic cloves, crushed
- 4 tbsp butter
- 3 cups fish stock

Spices:
- 2 tbsp fresh parsley, finely chopped
- 1 tsp salt
- ¼ tsp onion powder
- ¼ tsp garlic powder
- ¼ tsp dried oregano

Directions:

1. Place greens in a large colander and rinse under cold running water. Drain well and set aside.
2. Chop broccoli and onions. Set aside.
3. Plug in the instant pot and grease the inner pot with butter. Heat up and add onions and garlic. Cook for 2-3 minutes and then add tomatoes. Continue to cook for another 3-4 minutes.
4. Now add broccoli and season with salt, garlic powder, onion powder, and oregano. Stir well and pour in about ¼ cup of the stock. Bring it to a boil and simmer for 4-5 minutes. Stir occasionally.
5. Press the "Cancel" button and add the remaining ingredients. Stir well and seal the lid.
6. Set the steam release handle to the "Sealing" position and press the "Manual" button.
7. Set the timer for 15 minutes on high pressure.
8. When done, release the pressure naturally and open the lid. Transfer the stew to serving bowls and optionally sprinkle with grated Parmesan cheese or some more fresh parsley.

Per Serving:
(Calories 312 | Total Fats 15.3g | Net Carbs: 8.7g | Protein: 32.1g | Fiber: 2.9g)

Spicy Trout with Broccoli

(TotalTime: 50 MIN | Serves: 5)

Ingredients:

- 2 lbs trout fillets, skin-on
- 3 cups broccoli, chopped
- 1 small onion, finely chopped
- ¼ cup olive oil
- 2 tbsp butter
- 2 tbsp apple cider vinegar
- 4 cups fish stock

Spices:
- ½ tsp salt
- ½ tsp dried celery
- 1 tsp chili powder
- ½ tsp chili flakes
- ¼ tsp garlic powder

Directions:

1. Remove the fish from the refrigerator about an hour before using. Rub with olive oil and sprinkle with salt, dried celery, chili powder, chili flakes, and garlic powder. Place in a deep bowl and cover with a lid. Set aside.
2. Plug in the instant pot and pour in the fish stock. Add broccoli and stir well. Seal the lid and set the steam release handle to the "Sealing" position. Set the timer for 20 minutes.
3. When done, perform a quick pressure release and open the lid. Remove the cauliflower from the pot and drain. Place in a deep bowl and mash with a potato masher. Optionally, transfer to a food processor and process until smooth. Set aside.
4. Place the steam insert in the pot and place the fish in it. Pour in 2 cups of water and seal the lid. Set the steam release handle again and press the "Fish" button.
5. When done, perform a quick pressure release and open the lid. Remove the fish from the pot and press the "Sauté" button.
6. Add mashed broccoli and stir in the butter. Optionally, sprinkle with some salt and garlic powder. Heat up and remove from the pot.
7. Serve with steamed fish.

Per Serving:
(Calories 488 | Total Fats 27.2g | Net Carbs: 3.3g | Protein: 54.2g | Fiber: 1.7g)

King Prawn Stew with Avocado

(Total Time: 45 MIN | Serves: 6)

Ingredients:

- 2 lbs king prawns, whole
- 7 oz cauliflower, chopped into florets
- 1 avocado, chopped into bite-sized pieces
- 2 small tomatoes, roughly chopped
- 1 small onion, finely chopped
- 2 large celery stalks, chopped
- 1 cup olive oil
- 4 tbsp balsamic vinegar
- 5 cups fish stock

Spices:
- 1 tsp sea salt
- 1 tsp dried marjoram
- ½ tsp dried thyme
- 1 tsp chili flakes

Directions:

1. Place prawns in a large colander and rinse well. Set aside.
2. In a medium-sized bowl, combine together oil, balsamic vinegar, salt, marjoram, thyme, and chili flakes. Stir well and add prawns. If necessary, add some fish stock to the bowl and submerge prawns in this mixture. Refrigerate for 20 minutes.
3. Meanwhile, prepare the vegetables and plug in the Instant pot. Press the "Sauté" button and add onions and celery stalks. Drizzle with some oil and cook for 4-5 minutes. Now add avocado, cauliflower, and tomatoes. Stir well and continue to cook for another 5 minutes.
4. Remove the prawns from the refrigerator and transfer to the pot. Press the "Cancel" button and pour in the remaining stock. Stir well and seal the lid.
5. Set the steam release handle and press the "Manual" button. Set the timer for 15 minutes.
6. When you hear the end signal, perform a quick pressure release and carefully open the lid.
7. Transfer the stew to serving bowls and optionally sprinkle with some pepper.
8. Serve immediately.

Per Serving:
(Calories 593 | Total Fats 44.4g | Net Carbs: 5.9g | Protein: 40.7g | Fiber: 4g)

Seafood

Chili Hake Fillets

(TotalTime: 45 MIN | Serves: 6)

Ingredients:

- 2 lbs hake fillets, skinless
- ½ cup olive oil
- ¼ cup apple cider vinegar
- 1 red onion, finely chopped
- 3 garlic cloves, minced
- ¼ cup soy sauce
- 3 cups fish stock

Spices:
- 2 tsp fresh rosemary
- 1 tsp sea salt
- 2 tbsp fresh dill, finely chopped
- 2 tsp chili powde

Directions:

1. Rinse fillets under cold running water and place them in a deep bowl. Drizzle with olive oil and apple cider vinegar. Sprinkle with rosemary, salt, dill, and chili powder. Cover with the lid and set aside.
2. Plug in the instant pot and grease the inner pot with some oil. Press the "Sauté" button and add onions and garlic. Stir-fry for 3-4 minutes and season with some salt and optionally some pepper.
3. Remove the fillets from the bowl and place in the pot. Drizzle with about two tablespoons of the marinade and pour in the stock. Seal the lid and set the steam release handle.
4. Press the "Manual" button and set the timer for 12 minutes on HIGH pressure.
5. When done, perform a quick release and carefully open the lid. Press the "Sauté" button and pour in the soy sauce.
6. Gently stir again and cook for 3-4 minutes.
7. Turn off the pot and serve immediately.

Per Serving:
(Calories 468 | Total Fats 30.6g | Net Carbs: 2.6g | Protein: 43.9g | Fiber: 0.5g)

Seafood

Mussel Chowder

(TotalTime: 30 MIN| Serves: 4)

Ingredients:

- 1 lb fresh mussels, cleaned
- 2 large onions, finely chopped
- 1 cup celery stalk, chopped
- 2 cups cauliflower, chopped into florets
- ¼ cup olive oil
- 5 cups fish stock
- 1 cup heavy cream
- ¼ cup Parmesan cheese, grated
- 2 tbsp fresh parsley, finely copped

Spices:
- 1 tsp sea salt
- ¼ tsp of chili flakes
- ½ tsp white pepper, freshly ground

Directions:

1. Rinse mussels and drain in a large sieve. Place in a deep pot and drizzle with some olive oil. Sprinkle with chili flakes and white pepper. Mix well and set aside,
2. Plug in the instant pot and press the "Sauté" button. Heat the remaining oil in the instant pot and add onions and chopped celery stalks. Stir well and cook for 5-6 minutes.
3. Now add cauliflower and continue to cook for another 2 minutes.
4. Finally, add mussels and pour in the fish stock. Press the "Cancel" button to turn off the pot.
5. Seal the lid and set the steam release handle to the "Sealing" position. Press the "Manual" button and set the timer for 8 minutes on high pressure.
6. When done, perform a quick release and open the lid. Stir in the heavy cream and divide the chowder between serving bowls.
7. Sprinkle with grated Parmesan and chopped parsley. Serve immediately.

Per Serving:
(Calories 428| Total Fats 30.3g | Net Carbs: 12.5g | Protein: 25g |Fiber: 3.3g)

Seafood

Salmon Fillet with Dill

(TotalTime: 15 MIN| Serves: 4)

Ingredients:

- 4 pieces salmon fillet, about 2 lbs
- ¼ cup apple cider vinegar
- 1 cup fresh dill, finely chopped
- 1 tbsp butter, unsalted

Spices:
- 1 tsp salt
- ¼ tsp black pepper, freshly ground

Directions:

1. Plug in the instant pot and set the steam basket in the inner pot. Pour in one cup of water and apple cider in the inner pot and set aside.
2. Rinse the salmon fillets and sprinkle with salt and pepper. Place in the steam basket and top with fresh dill.
3. Seal the lid and set the steam release handle to the "Sealing" position. Press the "Steam" button and set the timer for 9 minutes.
4. When done, perform a quick pressure release and open the lid. Remove the salmon and set aside.
5. Now press the "Sauté" button and grease the inner pot with butter. Heat up and briefly brown salmon on both sides – for about 2 minutes.
6. Top with some more fresh dill before serving.

Per Serving:
(Calories 359| Total Fats 17.4g | Net Carbs: 5.2g | Protein: 46.4g |Fiber: 1.6g)

Seafood

Wild Alaskan Cod with Cherry Tomatoes

(TotalTime: 20 MIN | Serves: 4)

Ingredients:

- 2 lbs wild Alaskan cod fillets
- 1 cup cherry tomatoes
- 2 garlic cloves, crushed
- 2 tbsp butter
- 3 tbsp olive oil

Spices:
- 1 tsp salt
- ½ tsp black pepper, freshly ground
- ½ tsp rosemary powder
- ½ tsp dried thyme

Directions:

1. Rinse the fillets under cold running water and pat-dry with a kitchen towel. Place on a cutting board and cut into 4 equal pieces.
2. In a large mixing bowl, combine tomatoes, garlic, salt, pepper, rosemary, and thyme. Stir until well combined and set aside.
3. Plug in the instant pot and pour two cups of water in the inner pot. Position a trivet on the bottom of the pot and set aside.
4. Line a round 7-inch baking dish with some parchment paper and place the fillets in it. Generously brush with olive oil and pour in the tomato mixture. Place the dish in the pot and seal the lid.
5. Set the steam release handle to the "Sealing" position and press the "Manual" button. Cook for 10 minutes on high pressure.
6. When done, press the "Cancel" button and perform a quick release. Open the pot and carefully remove the baking dish.
7. Chill for a while and serve. Optionally, sprinkle with some more salt or pepper to taste.

Per Serving:
(Calories 354 | Total Fats 17.5g | Net Carbs: 1.7g | Protein: 45.6g | Fiber: 0.6g)

Seafood

Tiger Prawn Paella

(Total Time: 25 MIN | Serves: 4)

Ingredients:

- 1 lb tiger prawns, whole
- 2 cups cauliflower, chopped into florets
- 1 small red bell pepper, finely chopped
- 4 cups fish stock
- 1 tsp apple cider vinegar
- 2 small onion, finely chopped
- 3 garlic cloves, crushed
- 5 bacon slices, chopped
- 3 tbsp butter

Spices:
- 4 tbsp fresh parsley, finely chopped
- 1 tsp sea salt
- ½ tsp black pepper, freshly ground
- 2 tsp turmeric powder
- ½ tsp saffron threads

Directions:

1. Plug in the instant pot and add cauliflower. Pour in the fish stock and sprinkle with salt. Seal the lid and set the steam release handle to the "Sealing" position. Press the "Manual" button and set the timer for 5 minutes on high pressure.
2. When done, perform a quick release and open the lid. Remove the cauliflower from the pot and drain. Make sure to reserve the stock. Set aside.
3. Press the "Sauté" button and grease the inner pot with butter. Heat up and add onions and garlic. Stir-fry for 4-5 minutes.
4. Now add bell pepper and bacon. Continue to cook for another 3-4 minutes, stirring constantly. Season with some more salt, pepper, and turmeric powder.
5. Stir well and add prawns and cauliflower. Pour in the remaining stock and seal the lid.
6. Set the steam release handle again and press the "Manual" button. Set the timer for 8 minutes on high pressure.
7. When done, release the pressure naturally and open the lid. Stir well and sprinkle with saffron and fresh parsley. Let it sit for a while before serving.
8. Optionally, press the "Sauté" button again and gently simmer until all the liquid evaporates.

Per Serving:
(Calories 419 | Total Fats 22.6g | Net Carbs: 8.5g | Protein: 41.8g | Fiber: 2.5g)

Seafood

Simple Squid Stew

(TotalTime: 40 MIN | Serves: 4)

Ingredients:

- 7 oz squid rings, defrosted
- 7 oz shrimps, cleaned
- 1 medium-sized yellow bell pepper, sliced
- 1 small onion, finely chopped
- 1 cup cabbage, shredded
- 2 cups cherry tomatoes, diced
- 3 cups fish stock
- ¼ cup olive oil

Spices:
- 2 tsp pink Himalayan salt
- ½ tsp dried oregano
- 1 tsp rosemary powder
- 1 tsp stevia powder

Directions:

1. Grease the inner pot with some olive oil and heat up on the "Sauté" mode. Add onions and stir-fry until translucent. Now add bell pepper and season with salt. Stir well and continue to cook for another 2 minutes.
2. Stir in tomatoes and add about ¼ cup of the stock. Simmer until the liquid evaporates and press the "Cancel" button.
3. Finally, add the remaining ingredients and season with oregano, rosemary, and stevia powder. Stir well and seal the lid.
4. Set the steam release handle to the "Sealing" position and press the "Manual" button set the timer for 20 minutes on high pressure.
5. When done, perform a quick release and open the lid. Divide between serving plates and optionally sprinkle with some Parmesan.
6. Serve immediately.

Per Serving:
(Calories 279 | Total Fats 15.8g | Net Carbs: 8.4g | Protein: 24.5g | Fiber: 2.3g)

Seafood

Creamy Shrimp Stew

(TotalTime: 35 MIN | Serves: 4)

Ingredients:

- 1 lb shrimps, peeled and deveined
- 3 bacon slices, chopped
- 1 cup onion, finely chopped
- ¼ cup bell peppers, diced
- 1 cup cherry tomatoes, sliced in half
- ½ cup heavy cream
- ¼ cup scallions, chopped
- 2 cups fish stock
- 4 tbsp olive oil

Spices:
- 1 tsp Old Bay seasoning
- 2 tsp apple cider vinegar
- ½ tsp garlic powder
- ½ tsp salt
- ¼ tsp white pepper, freshly ground

Directions:

1. Plug in the instant pot and press the "Sauté" button. Grease the inner pot with olive oil and add bacon. Cook for 3-4 minutes or until lightly golden brown and crisp. Remove the bacon from the pot and set aside.
2. Now add onions and bell peppers. Cook until translucent and add cherry tomatoes and scallions. Continue to cook for 10 minutes, stirring occasionally. If necessary, pour in some of the stock.
3. Now add shrimps and give it a good stir. Pour in the remaining stock and season with Old Bay seasoning, garlic powder, salt, and pepper. Sprinkle with some apple cider and seal the lid.
4. Set the steam release handle to the "Sealing" position and press the "Manual" button. Cook for 8 minutes on high pressure.
5. When done, release the pressure naturally and open the lid. Serve immediately.

Per Serving:
(Calories 427 | Total Fats 28.5g | Net Carbs: 6.4g | Protein: 35g | Fiber: 1.4g)

Seafood

Salmon Steaks with Cheese

(TotalTime: 20 MIN| Serves: 4)

Ingredients:

- 2 medium-sized salmon steaks, about 1 lb
- ½ cup Feta cheese
- 1 cup mozzarella, shredded
- ¼ cup heavy cream
- 2 cups vegetable stock
- 3 tbsp olive oil
- 2 tbsp butter

Spices:
- 1 tsp smoked paprika
- ½ tsp salt
- ½ tsp red pepper flakes
- 2 tbsp fresh parsley, finely chopped

Directions:

1. Rinse well the steaks and dry with a kitchen towel. Sprinkle with red pepper flakes and salt. Set aside.
2. Plug in the instant pot and press the "Sauté" button. Heat the olive oil and add salmon steaks. Briefly brown, for 2-3 minutes, on both sides and pour in the stock.
3. Season with smoked paprika and seal the lid.
4. Set the steam release handle to the "Sealing" position and press the "Manual" button.
5. Set the timer for 4 minutes on high pressure.
6. When done, perform a quick release and open the lid. Remove salmon steaks and the remaining stock.
7. Press the "Sauté" button again and melt the butter. Add Feta cheese, mozzarella, and heavy cream. Optionally, season with some chili flakes and give it a good stir.
8. Briefly cook – for a couple of minutes, stirring constantly.
9. Add salmon and coat well with the sauce. Serve immediately.

Per Serving:

(Calories 389| Total Fats 31.3g | Net Carbs: 1.4g | Protein: 27.1g |Fiber: 0.3g)

Sour King Scallops

(TotalTime: 20 MIN | Serves: 4)

Ingredients:

- 5 king scallops, fresh
- 1 medium-sized onion, finely chopped
- ¼ cup apple cider vinegar
- 1 cup fish stock
- 2 tbsp olive oil
- 3 tbsp butter
- 1 tbsp fresh lemon juice

Spices:
- 1 tsp salt
- ½ tsp garlic powder
- ½ tsp white pepper, freshly ground

Directions:

1. Plug in the instant pot and grease the inner pot with olive oil. Heat up and add onions. Cook for 3-4 minutes, or until translucent.
2. Pour in the stock and apple cider vinegar. Add scallops and gently simmer for 5 minutes.
3. Season with salt, garlic powder, and white pepper. Give it a good stir and press the "Cancel" button.
4. Seal the lid and set the steam release handle. Press the "Manual" button and set the timer for 8 minutes.
5. When done, perform a quick pressure release and open the lid.
6. Stir in the butter and sprinkle with lemon juice.
7. Serve immediately.

Per Serving:
(Calories 389 | Total Fats 31.3g | Net Carbs: 1.4g | Protein: 27.1g | Fiber: 0.3g)

Seafood

Sweet Broccoli Fish Stew

(TotalTime: 25 MIN| Serves: 3)

Ingredients:

- 1 lb trout fillets, defrosted and thinly sliced
- 1 cup broccoli, chopped
- ¼ cup soy sauce
- 1 cup fish stock
- 3 tbsp apple cider vinegar
- 1 tbsp arrowroot starch
- 2 tbsp butter
- 1 tbsp garlic paste
- ¼ cup spring onions, finely chopped

Spices:
- ½ tsp stevia extract
- 1 tsp marjoram, dried

Directions:

1. Rinse the broccoli under cold running water and drain in a large colander. Cut into florets and set aside.
2. Plug in the instant pot and pour in 1 cup of water. Set the steam basket and place broccoli in it.
3. Seal the lid and press the "Steam" button. Cook on high pressure.
4. When you hear the end signal, perform a quick pressure release and open the lid. Carefully remove the steam basket and chill for a while.
5. Now press the "Sauté" button and grease the inner pot with butter. Add trout and cook for 4-5 minutes. Gently turn over and continue to cook for another 3-4 minutes. Remove from the pot.
6. Now, pour in the stock, soy sauce, and apple cider vinegar. Bring it to a boil and stir in the garlic paste. Sprinkle with stevia and marjoram and cook for 30 seconds.
7. Add trout fillets and broccoli and toss well to coat with the sauce.
8. Finally, add the arrowroot starch and cook for 1 minute.
9. Press the "Cancel" button and serve immediately.

Per Serving:
(Calories 404| Total Fats 21.3g | Net Carbs: 5g | Protein: 44.6g |Fiber: 1.3g)

Seafood

5-Minute Mussels Soup

(TotalTime: 5 MIN| Serves: 3)

Ingredients:

- 7 oz mussels, defrosted and cleaned
- ¼ cup fish sauce
- 4 cups fish stock
- 1 cup cherry tomatoes, chopped
- 2 tbsp butter

Spices:
- 2 tsp Italian seasoning
- ¼ tsp stevia powder

Directions:

1. Rinse well and clean the mussels. Drain in a large sieve and place in the pot.
2. Sprinkle with Italian seasoning and stevia extract. Pour in the fish stock and soy sauce and add cherry tomatoes. Stir well and seal the lid.
3. Set the steam release handle to the "Sealing" position and press the "Manual" button.
4. When done, perform a quick pressure release and open the lid. Stir in the fish sauce and serve immediately.
5. Optionally, sprinkle with freshly chopped parsley before serving.

Per Serving:
(Calories 404| Total Fats 21.3g | Net Carbs: 5g | Protein: 44.6g |Fiber: 1.3g)

Seafood

Lobster Tails in Butter Sauce

(TotalTime: 15 MIN| Serves: 4)

Ingredients:

- 1 lb fresh lobster tails, cleaned
- ¼ cup fish stock
- 1 tbsp apple cider vinegar
- ½ cup mayonnaise
- 5 tbsp butter, unsalted
- 1 cup water

Spices:
- 1 tsp salt
- ½ tsp black pepper, freshly ground
- ¼ tsp dried thyme
- ¼ tsp dried rosemary
- ¼ tsp garlic powder

Directions:

1. Place lobster tails in the steam basket and transfer to the pot. Pour in one cup of water and seal the lid. Set the steam release handle to the "Sealing" position and press the "Steam" button. Cook for 5 minutes on high pressure.
2. When done, preform a quick pressure release and open the lid. Remove the lobster tails from the pot and press the "Sauté" button.
3. Pour in the stock and bring it to a boil. Stir in butter and mayonnaise and sprinkle with apple cider.
4. Season with salt, pepper, thyme, rosemary, and garlic powder. Cook for 2-3 minutes.
5. Press the "Cancel" button and remove the sauce from the pot. Drizzle over steamed lobster tails and serve immediately.
6. Optionally, sprinkle with fresh dill.

Per Serving:
(Calories 347| Total Fats 25.3g | Net Carbs: 7.1g | Protein: 22.3g |Fiber: 0g)

Seafood

Steamed Mussels with Thyme

(TotalTime: 20 MIN| Serves: 4)

Ingredients:

- 1 lb mussels, cleaned
- 2 cups fish stock
- 5 garlic cloves, crushed
- 2 tbsp lemon juice, freshly squeezed
- 3 tbsp butter
- ¼ cup Parmesan cheese, grated

Spices:
- 1 tsp dried thyme
- ½ tsp chili flakes
- 2 tbsp fresh parsley, finely chopped

Directions:

1. Rinse well the mussels under running water and remove any dirt. Drain and set aside.
2. Plug in the instant pot and press the "Sauté" button. Grease the inner pot with butter and add garlic. Sauté for 2-3 minutes and then pour in the stock. Drizzle with lemon juice and season with thyme, chili flakes, and parsley.
3. Place mussels in a steam basket and transfer to the pot. Seal the lid and set the steam release handle to the "Sealing" position.
4. Press the "Manual" button and set the timer for 5 minutes on high pressure.
5. When done, perform a quick release and open the lid. Remove any mussels that didn't open and transfer to serving bowls. Drizzle with the sauce from the pot and serve immediately. .

Per Serving:
(Calories 207| Total Fats17.1g | Net Carbs: 5.6g | Protein: 17.1g |Fiber: 0.1g)

Chapter 5

Poultry

Ginger Chicken with Vegetables

(TotalTime: 30 MIN| Serves: 4)

Ingredients:

- 4 large chicken thighs, skin on
- 1 large tomato, roughly chopped
- 1 small onion, finely chopped
- 1 cup broccoli, chopped
- 1 cup spinach, torn
- 1 cup shiitake mushrooms, chopped
- 4 garlic cloves, crushed
- ¼ cup Dijon mustard
- 3 cups chicken stock
- 4 tbsp butter
- ¼ cup olive oil

Spices:
- 2 tsp sea salt
- 1 tbsp fresh mint, finely chopped
- 2 tbsp fresh ginger, grated
- 1 tbsp cayenne pepper

Directions:

1. In a small bowl, whisk together olive oil, Dijon mustard, garlic, salt, min, ginger, and cayenne pepper. Set aside.
2. Rinse each piece of chicken under cold running water and pat dry with some kitchen paper. Generously brush with the marinade and place in a bowl. Let it sit for a while.
3. Now plug in the instant pot and press the "Sauté" button. Grease the inner pot with butter and heat up. Add onion and cook for 2 minutes.
4. Now add tomatoes and mushrooms. Continue to cook for another 3 minutes. Finally, add the remaining vegetables and give it a good stir.
5. Add the chicken thighs and pour in the stock. Seal the lid and set the steam release handle to the "Sealing" position.
6. Press the "Meat" button.
7. When done, release the pressure naturally and open the lid. Serve immediately.

Per Serving:

(Calories 578 | Total Fats 31.6g | Net Carbs: 9.6g | Protein: 61.5g | Fiber: 3g)

Cauliflower Turkey Risotto

(Total Time: 30MIN | Serves: 3)

Ingredients:

- 1 lb turkey breast, chopped into bite-sized pieces
- 1 cup cauliflower florets, finely chopped
- ½ cup feta cheese
- 3 tbsp Parmesan, freshly grated
- 3 tbsp butter
- 3 cups chicken stock

Spices:
- 1 tsp salt
- ½ tsp black pepper, freshly ground

Directions:

1. Using a sharp cutting knife, cut the meat into smaller pieces and remove the skin (if any). Rub with salt and pepper. Place in your instant pot and pour in the stock.
2. Seal the lid and set the steam release handle. Press the "Meat" function and cook for 12 minutes.
3. When done, perform a quick release and open the lid. Remove the meat from the pot and place in a deep bowl. Set aside.
4. Remove the remaining stock and press the "Sauté" button. Grease the inner pot with butter and heat up.
5. Now add finely chopped cauliflower and sprinkle with some more salt and pepper. Pour in about ¼ cup of the stock and simmer for 10 minutes.
6. Now add the meat and stir well. Continue to cook for another 5 minutes.
7. Finally, stir in feta cheese and divide the mixture between serving plates. Sprinkle with grated Parmesan and serve immediately.

Per Serving:
(Calories 465 | Total Fats: 27g | Net Carbs: 2.1g | Protein: 51.6g | Fiber: 0g)

Creamy Chicken Wings with Peppers

(Total Time: 50MIN | Serves: 5)

Ingredients:

- 2 lbs chicken wings, whole
- 1 cup Brussels sprouts
- 1 green bell pepper
- 1 red bell pepper
- 7 oz Portobello mushrooms, sliced
- 1 cup heavy cream
- 3 tbsp sour cream
- ¼ cup olive oil
- 4 cups chicken stock

Spices:
- 2 tsp salt
- 1 tsp black pepper, freshly ground
- 1 tsp dried rosemary

Directions:

1. Plug in the instant pot and add sprouts in the stainless steel insert. Pour in three cups of water and add two tablespoons of olive oil. Sprinkle with some salt and seal the lid. Set the steam release handle to the "Sealing" position and press the "Manual" button. Set the timer for 10 minutes on high pressure.
2. When done, release the pressure by moving the pressure handle to the "Venting" position. Carefully open the lid and remove the sprouts from the pot. Drain and set aside.
3. Now rinse and clean each pepper. Cut in half and remove the seeds. Thinly slice and set aside.
4. Clean the mushrooms and slice each in half. Set aside.
5. Remove the stock from the pot and press the "Sauté" button. Grease the inner pot with the remaining olive oil and add the wings. Briefly brown each piece for 3-4 minutes on each side and remove from the pot.
6. Now add peppers and cook for 3 minutes stirring constantly. Season with some salt and add mushrooms. Continue to cook until the liquid evaporates.
7. Now add the meat and sprouts. Pour in the reserved stock as well as he remaining one cup. Season with salt, pepper, rosemary, and stir well.
8. Seal the lid and set the steam release handle to the "Sealing" position. Press the "Manual" button and set the timer for 15 minutes.
9. When done, perform a quick pressure release and open the lid.
10. Chill for a while and then stir in sour cream and heavy cream. Give it a good stir and optionally season with some more salt or pepper.
11. Serve immediately.

Per Serving:
(Calories 568 | Total Fats: 34.7g | Net Carbs: 6.4g | Protein: 56.1g | Fiber: 1.7g)

Poultry

Balsamic Chicken Breast with Basil

(TotalTime: 45MIN| Serves: 2)

Ingredients:

- 1 lb chicken breast, chopped into bite-sized pieces
- ½ cup balsamic vinegar
- 1 cup cherry tomatoes
- ½ cup fresh basil, finely chopped
- 2 cups chicken stock
- 3 tbsp butter
- 2 garlic cloves, whole

Spices:
- 1 tsp sea salt

Directions:

1. Rinse the meat under cold running water and pat dry with some kitchen paper. Place on a cutting board and chop into bite-sized pieces and transfer to a deep bowl. Pour in the balsamic vinegar and refrigerate for 20 minutes.
2. Meanwhile, plug in the instant pot and press the "Sauté" button. Melt the butter in the inner pot and add garlic. Briefly cook – for one minute and then add cherry tomatoes and basil. Give it a good stir and cook until tomatoes completely soften. Remove from the pot and transfer to a food processor. Process until smooth. Set aside.
3. Remove the chicken from the refrigerator and place in the pot. Pour in the stock and seal the lid. Set the steam release handle and press the 'Manual" button.
4. Set the timer for 10 minutes on high pressure.
5. When done, release the pressure naturally and open the lid. Stir in the tomato mixture and season with salt.
6. Optionally, add some pepper before serving.

Per Serving:
(Calories 456 | Total Fats: 23.8g | Net Carbs: 4.8g | Protein: 50.1g |Fiber: 1.2g)

Chicken Teriyaki

(TotalTime: 30MIN | Serves: 2)

Ingredients:

- 2 medium-sized chicken breast, cut in half lengthwise
- ¼ cup rice vinegar
- 2 tbsp balsamic vinegar
- 1 medium-sized onion, finely chopped
- ¼ cup soy sauce
- 3 tbsp olive oil

Spices:
- 1 tsp pink Himalayan salt
- 2 tsp red pepper flakes
- 1 tsp black pepper, freshly ground
- 1 tbsp ginger, freshly grated
- 1 tsp garlic powder

Directions:

1. Rinse well the meat and pat dry with a kitchen paper. Cut each piece in half, lengthwise and set aside.
2. In a large bowl, combine soy sauce, rice vinegar, balsamic vinegar, ginger, garlic, onions, pepper, red pepper flakes, and olive oil. Mix well and set aside.
3. Plug in the instant pot and add chicken. Pour in the soy mixture and about one cup of water. Securely lock the lid and set the steam release handle.
4. Press the "Manual" button and set the timer for 15 minutes on high pressure.
5. When done, release the pressure naturally and open the lid. Season with salt and stir well.
6. Optionally add some more pepper or red chili flakes. Stir well and serve.
7. For a thicker mixture, press the "Sauté" button again and simmer until a desired thickness.

Per Serving:
(Calories 370 | Total Fats: 23.9g | Net Carbs: 6.3g | Protein: 26.4g | Fiber: 1.4g)

Moroccan Risotto

(TotalTime: 35MIN | Serves: 2)

Ingredients:

- 1 lb chicken breast, boneless and skinless, cut into bite-sized pieces
- 1 spring onion, finely chopped
- 2 cups cauliflower, chopped into florets
- 2 cups chicken stock
- 3 tbsp olive oil

Spices:
- 1 tsp turmeric powder
- 1 tsp fresh oregano
- 1 pinch saffron
- 2 tsp salt
- ½ tsp white pepper

Directions:

1. Rinse well the meat and pat dry with a kitchen paper. Set aside.
2. Plug in the instant pot and press the "Sauté" button. Heat the inner pot and add olive oil and onions. Briefly cook, for 3-4 minutes.
3. Now add the remaining ingredients and stir well. Securely lock the lid and adjust the steam release handle. Press the "Manual" button. Set the timer for 15 minutes.
4. When you hear the end signal, release the pressure naturally and open the lid.
5. Transfer the mixture to a large platter and chop the cauliflower into small piece.
6. Sprinkle with some more saffron and serve immediately.

Per Serving:
(Calories 476 | Total Fats: 27.3g | Net Carbs: 3.9g | Protein: 50.9g | Fiber: 2.7g)

Chicken Fajitas

(TotalTime: 45 MIN | Serves: 4)

Ingredients:

- 1 lb chicken breast, chopped into bite-sized pieces
- 2 tbsp homemade taco seasoning
- 1 cup cherry tomatoes, chopped
- 3 garlic cloves, minced
- 1 bell pepper, cut into strips
- 1 onion, finely chopped
- 1 tbsp lime juice
- 6 large leaves Iceberg lettuce

For homemade taco seasoning:
- 3 tbsp chili powder
- 1 tsp onion powder
- 2 tbsp pink Himalayan salt
- 2 tsp garlic powder
- 2 tsp oregano
- 1 tbsp smoked paprika
- ½ tsp coriander powder
- ½ tsp black pepper, freshly ground

Directions:

1. Combine all ingredients for taco seasoning in a jar and shake well. Set aside.
2. Rinse well the meat and place in a deep bowl. Generously sprinkle with taco seasoning. Place in the pot and add tomatoes, garlic, sliced peppers, onions, and lime juice.
3. Seal the lid and press the "Poultry" button. Set the timer for 8 minutes on high pressure.
4. When done, perform a quick release and open the lid. Remove the mixture from the pot and place in a bowl. Cool completely.
5. Spread about 2-3 tablespoons of the mixture at the center of each lettuce leaf and wrap tightly. Secure each wrap with a toothpick and serve immediately.

Per Serving:

(Calories 322 | Total Fats: 6.1g | Net Carbs: 11.4g | Protein: 50.4g | Fiber: 3.2g)

Keto Piccata

(Total Time: 45 MIN | Serves: 4)

Ingredients:

- 4 chicken breast, boneless and skinless
- 1 cup chicken broth
- 2 tbsp butter
- ¼ cup apple cider vinegar
- 2 tbsp brined capers, drained
- 2 cups button mushrooms, sliced

Spices:
- ½ tsp salt
- ½ tsp black pepper, freshly ground
- 2 tbsp flat-leaf parsley, chopped

Directions:

1. Rinse the meat under cold running water and rub with salt and pepper.
2. Plug in the instant pot and press the "Sauté" button. Grease the inner pot with butter and heat up. Add the prepared chicken and briefly brown on all sides, for 2-3 minutes.
3. Press the "Cancel" button and pour in the broth. Seal the lid and press the "Manual" button. Set the timer for 15 minutes on high pressure.
4. When done, perform a quick pressure release and open the lid.
5. Remove the chicken from the pot and transfer to a deep bowl. Cover with the lid and or a large piece of aluminum foil and set aside.
6. Remove the broth from the instant pot and press the "Sauté" button. Add the apple cider vinegar, the remaining butter, capers, and parsley. Stir well and add mushrooms. Cook until mushrooms soften.
7. Finally, add chicken and give it a good stir. Serve immediately.

Per Serving:
(Calories 414 | Total Fats: 13.1g | Net Carbs: 1.1g | Protein: 68.1g | Fiber: 0.4g)

Chinese Simmered Chicken

(TotalTime: 45 MIN | Serves: 5)

Ingredients:

- 3 lbs chicken thighs, boneless and chopped into bite-size pieces
- 2 tbsp olive oil

For the sauce:
- 1/3 cup soy sauce
- 1/3 cup swerve
- ¼ cup water
- ¼ cup apple cider vinegar
- 1 tbsp tomato paste, sugar-free
- ½ tsp red chili flakes
- 2 garlic cloves, crushed
- 1 small onion, finely chopped
- 1 tsp toasted sesame seeds

Directions:

1. In a small bowl, whisk together all sauce ingredients. Set aside.
2. Rinse the meat and chop into smaller pieces.
3. Plug in the instant pot and grease the inner pot with oil. Press the "Sauté" button and heat the oil. Add chicken in several batches and brown on all sides for 3-4 minutes. Remove from the pot and transfer to a deep bowl. Set aside.
4. Pour in the sauce mixture and stir well. Cook for 2-3 minutes and then add the meat. Give it a good stir and continue to cook for another 10-12 minutes.
5. Press the "Cancel" button and remove from the pot.
6. Serve immediately.

Per Serving:
(Calories 590 | Total Fats: 26.1g | Net Carbs: 3.2g | Protein: 80.3g | Fiber: 0.7g)

Citrus Chicken Thighs

(TotalTime: 60MIN| Serves: 4)

Ingredients:

- 4 chicken thighs, skin on
- 1 cup chicken stock
- ¼ cup apple cider vinegar

For the marinade:
- 1 lemon, sliced
- ¼ cup lemon juice, freshly squeezed
- 2 garlic cloves, crushed
- 3 rosemary sprigs
- ½ cup fresh parsley leaves, finely chopped
- 2 sage sprigs
- 4 tbsp olive oil
- 1 tsp salt

Directions:

1. Mix together all marinade ingredients and set aside.
2. Rinse well the meat and generously brush with the marinade. Place in a large Ziploc bag and refrigerate for 30 minutes.
3. Plug in the instant pot and add chicken and about 2 tablespoons of the marinade. Pour in the chicken stock and apple cider vinegar.
4. Seal the lid and set the steam release handle to the "Sealing" position. Press the "Manual" button and set the timer for 15 minutes on high pressure.
5. When done, perform a quick release and open the lid. Press the "Sauté" button and continue to cook for another 7-8 minutes.
6. Press the "Cancel" button and serve immediately.

Per Serving:
(Calories 381 | Total Fats: 10.6g | Net Carbs: 0.6g | Protein: 66g | Fiber: 0.1g)

Cheesy Turkey

(TotalTime: 35MIN| Serves: 4)

Ingredients:

- 2 lbs turkey breasts
- 1 cup tomatoes, diced
- ½ cup cream cheese
- ½ cup cheddar cheese, grated
- ½ cup chicken stock
- 2 tbsp olive oil

Spices:
- 1 tbsp Italian seasoning
- ½ tsp salt
- ¼ tsp black pepper, ground
- ½ tsp dried thyme, ground

Directions:

1. Rinse the meat under cold running water and pat dry with a kitchen towel. Generously sprinkle with Italian seasoning, salt, pepper, and thyme.
2. Plug in your instant pot and grease the stainless steel insert with olive oil. Press "Sauté" button and add meat. Pour in the chicken stock and tomatoes. Securely close the lid and set the steam release handle to the "Sealing" position.
3. Press the "Poultry" button. The cooking time will depend on the type of the meat you're using. For the frozen breasts, add about 10 minutes to your cooking time.
4. When done, perform a quick pressure release and open the lid.
5. Transfer the meat to a clean work surface and cut into bite-sized pieces.
6. Preheat the oven to 400 degrees. Line some baking paper over a baking pan and set aside.
7. Place the meat onto a baking sheet and spread the cream cheese and cheddar cheese on top. Optionally, sprinkle with some red pepper flakes and parsley.
8. Place it in the oven and bake for 10 minutes.

Per Serving:
(Calories 378 | Total Fats: 24g | Net Carbs: 10.9g | Protein: 27.6g | Fiber: 1.3g)

Cajun Chicken Breast

(Total Time: 35 MIN | Serves: 4)

Ingredients:

- 1 lb boneless and skinless chicken breast, thinly sliced
- 3 tbsp olive oil
- 1 small onion, finely chopped
- 3 garlic cloves, crushed
- ¼ cup cherry tomatoes
- 2 cups cauliflower, chopped into florets
- 1 red bell pepper, sliced
- 2 cups chicken broth

Spices:
- 2 tsp pink Himalayan salt
- ½ tsp dried rosemary
- ¼ tsp dried thyme
- 2 tsp red pepper, freshly ground
- 2 tsp paprika
- 1 tsp onion powder
- ¾ tsp garlic powder

Directions:

1. Combine spices in a small jar and seal the lid. Shake well until completely combined and set aside.
2. Rinse well the chicken and place on a large cutting board. Using a sharp knife, thinly slice each piece and place in a deep bowl. Generously sprinkle with the Cajun mixture.
3. Plug in the instant pot and press the "Sauté" button. Grease the inner pot with olive oil and heat up.
4. Add onions and cook until translucent. Now add bell peppers, garlic, cherry tomatoes, and cauliflower. Stir well and continue to cook for 5 minutes.
5. Pour in the chicken broth and add the seasoned meat. Seal the lid and set the steam release handle.
6. Press the "Manual" button and set the timer for 10 minutes.
7. When done, perform a quick release of the pressure and carefully open the lid.
8. Serve immediately.

Per Serving:
(Calories 315 | Total Fats: 14.8g | Net Carbs: 6g | Protein: 37g | Fiber: 2.2g)

Shredded Chicken with Shiitake

(TotalTime: 30MIN | Serves: 5)

Ingredients:

- 6 shiitake mushrooms
- 1 lb chicken breast, boneless and skinless
- 1 ½ cup chicken stock
- 1 spring onion, finely chopped
- 4 tbsp sesame oil
- 2 tbsp butter
- 2 tbsp dark soy sauce
- 1 tbsp light soy sauce
- ½ tsp stevia powder
- 2 tsp rice vinegar

Spices:
- 1 tbsp fresh ginger, grated
- ½ tsp pepper, freshly ground
- ½ tsp chili flakes

Directions:

1. In a small bowl, whisk together oil, dark soy sauce, light soy sauce, stevia powder, rice vinegar, ginger, chili flakes, and pepper. Optionally, add some salt and set aside.
2. Rinse the meat and place on a cutting board. Chop into smaller pieces and place at the bottom of your instant pot. Add spring onions and pour in the stock.
3. Seal the lid and set the steam release handle to the "Sealing" position. Press the "Poultry" button and cook for 10 minutes.
4. When you hear the cooker's end signal, perform a quick pressure release and open the lid. Remove the chicken from the pot and place in a deep bowl. Drizzle with the prepared soy mixture and shred with two forks. Set aside.
5. Remove the remaining stock from the pot and press the "Sauté" button. Grease the inner pot with butter and heat up.
6. Add shiitake and briefly cook – for 3-4 minutes, stirring constantly.
7. Now add the meat and give it a good stir. Cook for another 5 minutes.
8. When done, remove from the pot and serve immediately.

Per Serving:

(Calories 299 | Total Fats: 18.1g | Net Carbs: 11.3g | Protein: 21.7g | Fiber: 2g)

Chicken Tostadas

(TotalTime: 20MIN | Serves: 2)

Ingredients:

- 2 large chicken breast, skinless and boneless
- 1 cup chicken stock
- 1 cup tomatoes, roughly chopped

Spices:
- 2 tsp chili powder
- ½ tsp white pepper, freshly ground
- 1 tsp salt
- 1 tsp smoked paprika
- ½ tsp garlic powder
- ¾ tsp onion powder
- ¼ tsp cayenne pepper
- ½ tsp cumin powder

Directions:

1. Rinse the chicken under cold running water and pat dry with a kitchen paper. Set aside.
2. Plug in the instant pot and add the chicken. Pour in the chicken stock and seal the lid. Set the steam release handle to the "Sealing" position and press the "Manual" button. Cook for 10 minutes on high pressure.
3. When you hear the end signal, release the pressure naturally and open the lid. Carefully transfer the chicken to a serving plate and cool to a room temperature.
4. Using two forks shred the chicken and place back to the pot. Add tomatoes and all spices.
5. Stir well and press the "Sauté" button. Cook for 3-4 minutes, stirring constantly.
6. When done, press the "Cancel" button and remove the meat from the pot. Serve immediately with your favorite toasted keto bread.

Per Serving:
(Calories 474 | Total Fats: 9.6g | Net Carbs: 2.8g | Protein: 88.1g | Fiber: 1.1g)

Teriyaki Chicken Thighs with Peppers

(Total Time: 70 MIN | Serves: 5)

Ingredients:

- 2 lbs chicken thighs, skin on
- 5 garlic cloves, crushed
- 2 red bell peppers, sliced
- 1 cup chicken stock
- 5 tbsp soy sauce
- ¼ cup rice vinegar
- 2 tbsp sesame oil
- 2 tbsp swerve

Spices:
- 1 tsp chili flakes
- ½ tsp white pepper, freshly ground
- 1 tsp salt

Directions:

1. First, you will have to prepare the teriyaki mixture. In a small bowl, whisk together sesame oil, rice vinegar, swerve, soy sauce, chili flakes, pepper, and salt. Set aside.
2. Rinse the thighs and pat dry with a kitchen towel. Generously brush with the teriyaki mixture and place in a large Ziploc bag. Seal the bag and refrigerate for 20 minutes.
3. Meanwhile, plug in the instant pot and press the "Sauté" button. Grease the inner pot with some oil and add garlic. Briefly cook, for one minute, and then add sliced pepper. Continue to cook for another couple of minutes.
4. Now add the meat along with teriyaki and briefly brown – for 2-3 minutes on each side. You will probably have to do this in several batches.
5. Now pour in the stock and seal the lid. Set the steam release handle and press the "Manual" button. Set the timer for 15 minutes on high pressure.
6. When done, release the pressure naturally and open the lid.
7. Meanwhile, preheat the oven to 400 degrees. Line a large baking sheet with some parchment paper and add the thighs.
8. Cook for 15 minutes, turning once.

Per Serving:

(Calories 431 | Total Fats: 19.1g | Net Carbs: 5.2g | Protein: 54.3g | Fiber: 0.8g)

Poultry

Turkey Breast with Gorgonzola Sauce

(TotalTime: 45 MIN | Serves: 5)

Ingredients:

- 1 lb turkey breast, chopped into bite-sized pieces
- 2 tbsp butter
- 2 tbsp oil
- 2 cups heavy cream
- ½ cup gorgonzola, chopped
- ¼ cup fresh parsley, finely chopped
- 1 ½ cup chicken broth

Spices:
- 1 tsp garlic powder
- ½ tsp onion powder
- ¼ tsp dried oregano
- 1 tsp dried thyme

Directions:

1. Rinse well the meat and pat dry with a kitchen towel. Place on a large cutting board and chop into bite-sized pieces. Transfer to a large bowl. Coat well with spices and set aside.
2. Plug in the instant pot and press the "Sauté" button. Grease the inner pot with oil and add the meat. Briefly cook for 4-5 minutes, stirring constantly and pour in the broth. Press the "Cancel" button and seal the lid.
3. Set the steam release handle to the "Sealing" position and press the "Manual" button. Cook for 13 minutes on high pressure.
4. When done, release the pressure naturally for 10-15 minutes and then move the pressure valve to the "Venting" position to release any remaining pressure.
5. Open the lid and remove any remaining broth. Press the "Sauté" button and add butter.
6. Stir in heavy cream and gorgonzola. Sauté for a couple of minutes or until the cheese melts.
7. Sprinkle with parsley and serve immediately.

Per Serving:
(Calories 480 | Total Fats: 37.6g | Net Carbs: 2.3g | Protein: 32.9g | Fiber: 0.6g)

Turkey Breast with Garlic Gravy

(Total Time: 40 MIN | Serves: 6)

Ingredients:

- 3 lbs turkey breast, boneless and skinless
- 2 cups chicken stock
- 1 large onion, finely chopped
- 1 celery stalk, finely chopped
- 4 tbsp butter
- 3 garlic cloves, crushed

Spices:
- 1 thyme sprig, whole
- 1 sea salt
- ½ tsp garlic powder
- 1 tsp onion powder
- ¼ smoked paprika

Directions:

1. In a small bowl, combine salt, garlic powder, onion powder, and smoked paprika. Set aside.
2. Rinse the meat and place on a clean work surface. Using a sharp knife, slice each piece lengthwise to create a pocket. Stuff each with celery, garlic, and onions. Generously run with spices and transfer to the pot.
3. Pour in the stock and add thyme sprig. Seal the lid and set the steam release handle to the "Sealing" position.
4. Press the "Manual" button and set the timer for 20 minutes on high pressure.
5. When done, release the pressure naturally and open the lid. Stir in the butter and let it sit, covered, for a while before serving.

Per Serving:
(Calories 320 | Total Fats: 11.7g | Net Carbs: 10.9g | Protein: 39.3g | Fiber: 1.8g)

Simple Turkey Stew

(Total Time: 30 MIN | Serves: 5)

Ingredients:

- 2 lbs turkey breast, chopped into smaller pieces
- 4 cups chicken broth
- 2 celery stalks, chopped
- 4 tbsp butter
- 1 onion, finely chopped
- 2 cups cherry tomatoes, chopped
- ¾ cup heavy cream

Spices:
- 2 tsp salt
- 1 tsp peppercorn
- 1 tsp dried thyme

Directions:

1. Combine the ingredients in the instant pot and seal the lid.
2. Set the steam release handle to the "Sealing" position and press the "Stew" button. Set the timer for 20 minutes on high heat.
3. When done, release the pressure naturally and open the lid. Chill for a while and stir in some sour cream.
4. Serve immediately.

Per Serving:
(Calories 386 | Total Fats: 20.1g | Net Carbs: 11.5g | Protein: 36.2g | Fiber: 2.4g)

Turkey Meatballs in Sweet Sauce

(Total Time: 35MIN | Serves: 4)

Ingredients:

- 1 lb ground turkey meat
- 5 tbsp almond flour
- 3 tbsp butter
- 3 large eggs
- 2 tbsp olive oil
- ¼ cup soy sauce
- ¼ tsp rice vinegar
- ½ cup chicken stock
- 1 tbsp sesame seeds

Spices:

- 1 tsp salt
- ½ tsp black pepper
- 2 tsp stevia powder
- ¼ tsp garlic powder

Directions:

1. In a large bowl, combine ground turkey with almond flour, olive oil, and eggs. Season with some salt and pepper. Mix well until completely combined and shape balls –approximately 1-inch in diameter.
2. Plug in the instant pot and pour in 1 cup of water. Set the steam basket and place meatballs in it. Seal the lid and set the steam release handle to the "Sealing" position. Press the "Manual" button and cook for 10 minutes.
3. When you hear the end signal, perform a quick pressure release and open the lid. Remove the basket from the pot and set aside.
4. Remove the remaining water and press the "Sauté" button. Add butter and pour in the soy sauce, chicken stock and rice vinegar. Sprinkle with sesame seeds and the remaining spices. Stir well and add meatballs. Cook for 3-4 minutes.
5. Remove from the pot and serve immediately.

Per Serving:

(Calories 448 | Total Fats: 29.6g | Net Carbs: 2.4g | Protein: 41g | Fiber: 1.2g)

Turkey Leg with Garlic

(TotalTime: 55 MIN | Serves: 1)

Ingredients:

- 1 turkey leg
- 2 tbsp olive oil
- 3 tbsp light soy sauce
- 3 cups chicken stock
- 4 garlic cloves, crushed

Spices:
- 1 tbsp garlic paste
- 2 tsp oregano, dried
- 2 tsp dried thyme
- 1 tsp salt
- ¾ tsp white pepper, ground

Directions:

1. Combine together crushed garlic, garlic paste, oregano, thyme, salt, and pepper. Mix well and generously rub over turkey leg. Tightly wrap in a large piece of plastic foil and refrigerate for 30 minutes (up to an hour).
2. Remove from the refrigerator and place in the pot. Pour in the stock and seal the lid. Set the steam release handle to the "Sealing" position and press the "Manual" button.
3. Set the timer for 15 minutes on high pressure.
4. When done, perform a quick pressure release and open the lid. Remove the leg along with the stock from the pot and set aside.
5. Now grease the inner pot with olive oil and press the "Sauté" button. Place the leg back to the pot and pour in the soy sauce. Briefly brown for a couple of minutes on each side. Remove from the pot and serve.

Per Serving:
(Calories 629 | Total Fats: 39.7g | Net Carbs: 9.6g | Protein: 62.2g | Fiber: 0.3g)

Easy Turkey Roast

(TotalTime: 60MIN | Serves: 5)

Ingredients:

- 2 lbs turkey breast, boneless and skinless
- 3 tbsp garlic infused oil
- ¼ cup olive oil
- 3 tbsp Dijon mustard
- 4 cups chicken stock

Spices:
- 2 tsp sea salt
- 1 tsp white pepper, freshly ground

Directions:

1. Place the meat in the pot and add chicken stock. Seal the lid and set the steam release handle.
2. Press the "Manual" button and cook for 25 minutes. When done, perform a quick pressure release and open the lid. Remove the meat from the pot and set aside.
3. Preheat the oven to 425 degrees F. Line some parchment paper over a baking sheet and set aside.
4. In a small bowl, whisk together garlic infused oil, olive oil, Dijon, salt, and pepper. Brush the meat with this mixture and place on a baking sheet.
5. Roast for 15 minutes on each side.
6. Remove from the oven and serve immediately.

Per Serving:
(Calories 458 | Total Fats: 25.4g | Net Carbs: 0.9g | Protein: 54.1g | Fiber: 0.3g)

Chili Turkey Casserole

(TotalTime: 40 MIN | Serves: 4)

Ingredients:

- 1 lb turkey breast, sliced into half-inch thick slices
- 1 medium-sized onion, sliced
- 1 celery stalk, chopped
- 1 cup cauliflower, chopped
- 1 cup broccoli, chopped
- 1 chili pepper, sliced
- 1 cup cherry tomatoes, chopped
- 3 tbsp olive oil

Spices:
- 1 tsp salt
- 1 tsp black pepper, ground

Directions:

1. Season the meat with salt and pepper. Set aside.
2. Grease the bottom of a round baking pan with some oil. Add onions to create the first layer. Then add a layer of cauliflower and meat.
3. Add cherry tomatoes and finish with chili pepper and broccoli. Sprinkle with chopped celery and tightly wrap with aluminum foil.
4. Plug in the instant pot and set the trivet at the bottom of the inner pot. Pour in two cups of water and place the pan on top.
5. Seal the lid and set the steam release handle to the "Sealing" position and press the "Manual" button.
6. Set the timer for 20 minutes.
7. When done, perform a quick release of the pressure and open the lid.
8. Remove the aluminum foil and chill for a while.
9. Serve immediately.

Per Serving:
(Calories 242 | Total Fats: 12.6g | Net Carbs: 9.2g | Protein: 21.2g | Fiber: 3g)

Chapter 6
Beef & Lamb

Beef & Lamb

Beef Egg Casserole

(Total Time: 15 MIN | Serves: 3)

Ingredients:

- 1 lb ground beef
- 6 large eggs
- ¼ cup milk, full-fat
- ¼ cup mozzarella, crumbled
- 1 tbsp fresh parsley, finely chopped
- 1 tbsp olive oil

Spices:
- 1 tsp salt
- ½ tsp black pepper, ground
- ¼ tsp chili powder
- ¼ tsp dried rosemary, ground

Directions:

1. In a large mixing bowl, combine ground beef, mozzarella, milk, and parsley. Mix until well incorporated.
2. In a separate bowl, combine eggs and all the spices. Whisk until fluffy and pour over the meat mixture. Stir all well with a wooden spatula.
3. Grease a fitting oven-safe bowl with olive oil and add meat mixture. Gently press with your palm to flatten the surface and set aside.
4. Plug in your instant pot and pour 1 cup of water in the stainless steel insert. Position a trivet on the bottom and place the bowl on top.
5. Securely lock the lid and adjust the steam release handle. Press the "Manual" button and set the timer for 7 minutes. Cook on "High" pressure.
6. When you hear the cooker's end signal. Perform a quick pressure release and open the lid.
7. Carefully remove the bowl from the pot and serve immediately.
8. Optionally, top with sour cream or Greek yogurt.

Per Serving:

(Calories 483 | Total Fats 25g | Net Carbs: 2g | Protein 59.9g | Fiber: 0.3g)

Beef & Lamb

Italian Beef Chuck Roast

(Total Time: 45 MIN | Serves: 6)

Ingredients:

- 3 lbs beef chuck roast, boneless
- 5 garlic cloves, minced
- 1 tbsp butter
- 2 cups beef broth
- 1 cup tomatoes, diced
- 1 small onion, chopped

Spices:
- ½ tsp black pepper, ground
- 1 tsp sea salt
- 1 tsp fresh oregano, finely chopped
- ½ tsp dried basil, ground

Directions:

1. Rinse the meat under cold running water and pat dry with a kitchen paper. Transfer to a cutting board and cut into bite-sized pieces. Set aside.
2. Plug in your instant pot and add butter to the stainless steel insert. Press the "Sauté" button and gently melt. Add garlic and onions and cook for 3-4 minutes, or until onions translucent.
3. Add meat and cook for 5 minutes on each side.
4. Add tomatoes and all the spices. Pour in the broth and securely lock the lid. Set the steam release handle and press the "Manual" button. Set the timer for 25 minutes and cook on "High" pressure.
5. When you hear the cooker's end signal, release the pressure naturally.
6. Open the pot and transfer the meat to a serving plate.
7. Enjoy!

Per Serving:
(Calories 651 | Total Fats 49.2g | Net Carbs: 2.2g | Protein 46.2g | Fiber: 0.6g)

Beef & Lamb

Rosemary Beef Roast

(Total Time: 40 MIN | Serves: 6)

Ingredients:

- 2 lbs beef chuck roast, cut into large pieces
- 1 medium-sized red bell pepper, stripped
- ½ cup heavy cream
- 1 cup bone broth
- 3 garlic cloves, crushed
- 1 small onion, finely chopped
- 1 tsp balsamic vinegar
- 1 tsp olive oil

Spices:
- 1 tsp fresh rosemary, finely chopped
- 1 tsp salt
- 1 tsp black pepper, freshly ground
- 1 tsp dried marjoram, ground
- ½ tsp dried parsley, ground

Directions:

1. Plug in your instant pot and grease the stainless steel insert with olive oil. Press the "Sauté" button and add onions and garlic. Stir-fry for 3-4 minutes, or until translucent.
2. Add meat and generously sprinkle with salt. Cook for 3-4 minutes on each side, or until lightly browned. Now, add all the remaining ingredients and spices. Close the lid and adjust the steam release handle. Press the "Manual" button and set the timer for 25 minutes. Cook on "High" pressure.
3. When you hear the cooker's end signal, perform a quick release of the pressure and open the pot. Transfer all to a serving bowl and garnish with fresh rosemary before serving.

Per Serving:
(Calories 619 | Total Fats 46.7g | Net Carbs: 3g | Protein 43.6g | Fiber: 0.8g)

Chili Mushroom Beef Shank

(Total Time: 40 MIN | Serves: 4)

Ingredients:

- 2 lbs beef shank
- 1 cup button mushrooms, sliced
- 3 garlic cloves, minced
- 1 small green chili pepper, chopped
- 1 cup tomatoes, diced
- 2 cups beef broth
- 1 tbsp olive oil

Spices:
- 1 tbsp fresh ginger, grated
- 1 tsp salt
- 1 tsp dried thyme, ground
- ¼ tsp red chili flakes

Directions:

1. Rinse the meat under running water and pat dry with a kitchen towel. Rub with salt and pepper and set aside.
2. Plug in your instant pot and press the "Sauté" button. Grease the stainless steel with olive oil and add green chili and garlic. Cook for 2 minutes, stirring constantly.
3. Add mushrooms and cook for 5 minutes.
4. Now, add meat and sprinkle all with thyme, chili, and ginger. Give it a good stir and pour in the broth. Securely lock the lid and adjust the steam release handle.
5. Press the "Manual" button and set the timer for 25 minutes. Cook on "High" pressure.
6. When you hear the cooker's end signal, perform a quick pressure release and open the pot. Press the "Sauté" button and stir in the diced tomatoes. Cook for 5 minutes, stirring occasionally. Turn off the pot and transfer all to serving bowls.

Per Serving:
(Calories 492 | Total Fats 18.8g | Net Carbs: 3.6g | Protein 72.5g | Fiber: 1.1g)

Savory Cauliflower Beef Roast

(Total Time: 50 MIN | Serves: 6)

Ingredients:

- 2 lbs beef chuck roast, cut into small chunks
- 1 cup cauliflower, chopped
- 1 medium-sized onion, chopped
- 1 cup beef broth
- 2 tbsp butter
- ½ cup heavy cream
- 1 tbsp olive oil

Spices:
- 1 tsp sea salt
- ½ tsp black pepper, ground
- ½ tsp dried thyme, ground
- ¼ tsp dried rosemary, ground
- ½ tsp smoked paprika, ground

Directions:

1. Plug in your instant pot and grease the stainless steel insert with olive oil. Press the "Sauté" button and add the meat chunks and onions. Sprinkle with smoked paprika, salt, and pepper. Cook for 5 minutes, or until golden brown.
2. Pour in the beef broth and close the lid. Set the steam release handle by moving the valve to the "Sealing" position. Press the "Manual" button and set the timer for 25 minutes. Cook on "High" pressure.
3. When done, perform a quick release of the pressure by turning the valve to the "Venting" position.
4. Open the pot and press the "Sauté" button. Add cauliflower and heavy cream. Sprinkle with dried thyme and rosemary. Give it a good stir and bring it to a simmer. Cook for 10 minutes more, stirring occasionally.

Per Serving:
(Calories 657 | Total Fats 52.3g | Net Carbs: 2.3g | Protein 52.3g | Fiber: 1g)

Beef Steak in Balsamic Sauce

(Total Time: 30 MIN| Serves: 6)

Ingredients:

- 4 lbs beef steak
- ½ cup button mushrooms, sliced
- 1 cup balsamic vinegar
- 4 garlic cloves, finely chopped
- 1 small red onion, finely chopped
- 2 tbsp olive oil
- 1 cup bone broth
- ½ cup heavy cream

Spices:
- 2 tsp sea salt
- 1 tsp black peppercorns, whole
- 2 tsp fresh thyme, finely chopped
- 1 tsp fresh rosemary, finely chopped

Directions:

1. Rinse the meat under cold running water and transfer to a large bowl. Add balsamic vinegar, salt, thyme, peppercorns, and rosemary. Mix to combine and cover with an aluminum foil. Refrigerate for at least 30 minutes.
2. Plug in your in instant pot and grease the stainless steel insert with olive oil. Press the "Sauté" button and add mushrooms, garlic, and onions. Cook for 5 minutes, stirring occasionally. Add meat along with marinade and pour in the broth.
3. Securely lock the lid and press the "Manual" button. Set the timer for 15 minutes and cook on "High" pressure. When done, perform a quick pressure release and press the "Sauté" button again. Stir in the heavy cream and cook for 5 more minutes.
4. Transfer the meat to a serving platter and spoon over the balsamic sauce. Optionally, sprinkle with some finely chopped green onions or fresh parsley.

Per Serving:
(Calories 670 | Total Fats 27.3g | Net Carbs: 2.5g | Protein 95.8g | Fiber: 0.7g)

Chili Shoulder Roast

(Total Time: 45 MIN | Serves: 4)

Ingredients:

- 3 lbs beef shoulder roast
- 1 small red onion, finely chopped
- 1 medium-sized yellow bell pepper, chopped
- 3 garlic cloves, crushed
- 1 cup tomatoes, diced
- 2 cups beef broth
- 1 tbsp olive oil

Spices:
- 2 tsp sea salt
- 1 tsp red chili powder
- 1 tsp smoked paprika, ground
- 1 tsp dried oregano, ground
- 1 tsp dried basil, ground
- 1 tsp fresh rosemary, finely chopped

Directions:

1. Place the rinsed meat in a large bowl and generously rub with salt, chili powder, paprika, oregano, and basil. Set aside.
2. Plug in the instant pot and grease the stainless steel insert with olive oil. Press the "Sauté" button and add onions and bell peppers. Stir-fry for 3-4 minutes and add meat.
3. Cook for 5 minutes on each side, or until golden brown.
4. Add diced tomatoes and pour in the broth. Securely lock the lid and set the steam release handle. Press the "Manual" button and set the timer for 20 minutes. Cook on "High" pressure.
5. When you hear the cooker's end signal, perform a quick pressure release and open the pot. Carefully transfer the meat to a cutting board. Using two forks, shred and return the meat to the pot.
6. Press the "Sauté" button and cook until sauce thickens. Turn off the pot and stir in the fresh rosemary.
7. Serve warm.

Per Serving:

(Calories 595 | Total Fats 28.7g | Net Carbs: 5.8g | Protein 72.9g | Fiber: 2.1g)

Beef & Lamb

Grilled Beef Tenderloin

(Total Time: 35 MIN | Serves: 6)

Ingredients:

- 2 lbs beef tenderloin, cut into bite-sized pieces
- 4 garlic cloves, finely chopped
- 3 cups beef broth
- 1 tbsp olive oil
- 1 tbsp butter

Spices:
- 1 tsp onion powder
- 1 tsp dried oregano, ground
- 1 tsp dried rosemary, ground
- 1 tsp sea salt
- 1 tsp black pepper, ground

Directions:

1. Rinse the meat under running water and pat dry with a kitchen paper. Transfer to a cutting board and cut into bite-sized pieces. Place the meat chops in a large bowl and add all the spices. Generously rub with your hands to allow spice to penetrate into the meat. Set aside.
2. Plug in your instant and grease the stainless steel insert with olive oil. Press the "Sauté" button and add meat chops and garlic. Cook for 5 minutes, or until golden brown.
3. Now, pour in the beef broth and securely lock the lid. Adjust the steam release handle and press the "Manual" button. Set the timer for 20 minutes and cook on "High" pressure.
4. When you hear the cooker's end signal, perform a quick release of the pressure and open the pot. Transfer the meat to a serving platter and garnish with some finely chopped chives and fresh thyme before serving.

Per Serving:
(Calories 562 | Total Fats 28.3g | Net Carbs: 2.4g | Protein 69.7g | Fiber: 0.5g)

Beef & Lamb

Creamy Shiitake Beef Sirloin

(Total Time: 50 MIN | Serves: 6)

Ingredients:

- 2 lbs beef sirloin, cut into bite-sized pieces
- 1 cup Shiitake mushrooms, chopped
- 5 bacon slices, chopped
- 1 cup pearl onions, chopped
- 3 cups beef broth
- 1 cup heavy cream
- 1 tbsp butter

Spices:
- 1 tsp salt
- 1 tsp black pepper, freshly ground
- 1 tsp fresh sage, chopped
- 1 tsp fresh thyme, chopped

Directions:

1. Plug in your instant pot and press the "Sauté" button. Add chopped bacon and stir-fry for 2-3 minutes. Remove the bacon from the pot and set aside.
2. Add butter and gently melt, stirring constantly. Add mushrooms and onions. Cook for 5-7 minutes and remove from the pot.
3. Add meat and sprinkle with salt and pepper. Cook for 5 minutes and then pour in the broth. Close the lid and adjust the steam release handle. Press "Manual" button and set the timer for 25 minutes. Cook on "High pressure.
4. When done, perform a quick pressure release by moving the valve to the "Venting" position.
5. Open the pot and add mushroom mixture, bacon, and heavy cream. Press the "Sauté" button and bring it to a boil. Stir in the sage and thyme. Simmer for 10 more minutes. Turn off the pot and transfer all to a serving dish.

Per Serving:

(Calories 431 | Total Fats 18.8g | Net Carbs: 5.9g | Protein 55.1g | Fiber: 1.5g)

Beef & Lamb

Marinated Beef Shank

(Total Time: 40 MIN | Serves: 8)

Ingredients:

- 3 lbs beef shank
- 1 cup green onions
- 3 cups beef broth

For the marinade:
- 1 cup olive oil
- 2 garlic cloves, crushed
- 1 tbsp fresh rosemary, chopped
- 2 tsp fresh thyme, chopped
- 1 tsp salt
- 1 tsp black pepper, ground
- ½ tsp smoked paprika, ground

Directions:

1. In a large bowl, combine all marinade ingredients. Mix until well incorporated and set aside.
2. Rinse the meat under cold running water and pat dry with a kitchen paper. Place in a large Ziploc bag and pour in the marinade. Shake well to coat the meat evenly with the marinade. Refrigerate for 1 hour.
3. Plug in your instant pot and press the "Sauté" button. Drain the meat and place in the stainless steel insert. Cook for 5 minutes on each side, or until golden brown.
4. Pour in the broth and securely lock the lid. Adjust the steam release handle and press the "Manual" button. Set the timer for 20 minutes and cook on "High" pressure.
5. When you hear the cooker's end signal, release the pressure naturally.
6. Open the pot and transfer the meat to a serving plate. Drizzle with some marinade and garnish with green onions.

Per Serving:
(Calories 369 | Total Fats 14.7g | Net Carbs: 1.5g | Protein 53.8g | Fiber: 0.7g)

Butter Beef Roast

(Total Time: 55 MIN | Serves: 8)

Ingredients:

- 4 lbs beef roast
- ½ cup fresh cilantro, chopped
- 1 medium-sized red bell pepper, chopped
- 1 medium-sized onion, chopped
- 4 tbsp butter, divided
- 2 cups bone broth

Spices:
- 1 tsp dried oregano, ground
- 1 tsp dried rosemary, ground
- 1 tsp smoked paprika, ground
- 1 tsp sea salt
- 1 tsp black pepper, ground

Directions:

1. Plug in the instant pot and add 1 tablespoon of butter in the stainless steel insert. Gently stir until melt and add meat. Sprinkle with oregano, rosemary, paprika, salt, and pepper. Cook for 5-7 minutes on each side. Remove the meat to a large bowl and cover with a lid.
2. Now, add 1 more tablespoon of the butter to the pot. Add onions and red bell pepper and cook for 2-3 minutes.
3. Return the meat to the pot and slowly pour in the broth. Securely lock the lid and adjust the steam release handle.
4. Press the "Manual" button and set the timer for 20 minutes. Cook on "High" pressure.
5. When done, release the pressure naturally and open the pot. Press the "Sauté" button and stir in the remaining butter and cilantro. Simmer for 10-15 minutes more.
6. Press the "Cancel" button and turn off the pot. Transfer the meat to serving plate and slowly drizzle with the liquid from the pot.
7. Enjoy!

Per Serving:
(Calories 506 | Total Fats 20g | Net Carbs: 2.2g | Protein 74.3g | Fiber: 0.8g)

Mediterranean Beef Meatballs

(Total Time: 30 MIN | Serves: 6)

Ingredients:

- 2 lbs ground beef
- 1 cup fresh parsley, finely chopped
- ¼ cup feta cheese
- 1 medium-sized yellow bell pepper, chopped
- 3 large eggs
- 1 cup tomatoes, diced
- 1 small red onion, chopped
- 3 garlic cloves
- 1 cup beef broth
- 1 tbsp olive oil

Spices:
- 1 tsp sea salt
- ½ tsp red pepper flakes
- ½ tsp dried oregano, ground
- ¼ tsp dried thyme, ground

Directions:

1. In a large mixing bowl, combine beef, eggs, parsley, and cheese. Add about 1-2 tablespoons of lukewarm water mix with your hands. Add all the spices and mix until well incorporated.
2. Shape balls with the mixture, approximately 1-inch in diameter. Set aside,
3. Plug in your instant pot and grease the stainless steel insert with olive oil. Press the "Sauté" button and add onions and garlic. Stir-fry for 3-4 minutes, or until the onions translucent. Stir in the tomatoes and pour in the broth. Carefully place the meatballs in the pot and close the lid.
4. Adjust the steam release handle and press the "Manual" button. Set the timer for 10 minutes and cook on "High" pressure.
5. When you hear the cooker's end signal, perform a quick release of the pressure and open the pot.
6. Transfer the meatballs to a serving bowl and drizzle with the remaining sauce from the pot.
7. Optionally, brown the meatballs on each side before cooking in your instant pot.

Per Serving:
(Calories 383 | Total Fats 16.1g | Net Carbs: 4.3g | Protein 51.7g | Fiber: 1.4g)

Pepper Short Ribs

(Total Time: 40 MIN | Serves: 8)

Ingredients:

- 3 lbs beef short ribs
- 1 medium-sized red onion, diced
- 4 garlic cloves, crushed
- 1 cup heavy cream
- 2 cups beef stock

Spices:
- 1 tsp Italian seasoning
- 2 tsp black pepper, ground
- 1 tsp fresh thyme, chopped
- 1 tsp fresh sage, chopped

Directions:

1. Plug in the instant pot and add onions and garlic to the stainless steel insert. Cook for 3-4 minutes, or until onions translucent.
2. Add the ribs and pour in the broth. Sprinkle with Italian seasoning, thyme, and sage.
3. Close the lid and set the steam release handle by moving the valve to the "Sealing" position. Press the "Manual" button and set the timer for 20 minutes. Cook on "High" pressure.
4. When done, perform a quick pressure release and open the pot.
5. Stir in the heavy cream and press the "Sauté" button. Simmer for 10 more minutes.
6. Transfer the meat to a serving plate and drizzle over with the cream sauce.

Per Serving:
(Calories 416 | Total Fats 21.2g | Net Carbs: 2.3g | Protein 20.4g | Fiber: 21.2g)

Balsamic Fried Beef Roast

(Total Time: 25 MIN | Serves: 8)

Ingredients:

- 2 lbs beef chuck roast, cut into bite-sized pieces
- ½ cup shallots, chopped
- 3 garlic cloves, crushed
- ¼ cup balsamic vinegar
- ½ cup heavy cream
- 1 tbsp olive oil

Spices:
- 1 tsp salt
- 1 tsp dried oregano, ground
- 1 tsp black pepper, ground
- 1 tbsp dried parsley, finely chopped
- ¼ tsp dried marjoram, ground

Directions:

1. Rinse the meat under cold running water and pat dry with a kitchen towel. Transfer to a large cutting board and cut into bite-sized pieces. Rub with salt and pepper and set aside.
2. Grease the stainless steel insert of your instant pot with olive oil. Add shallots and garlic. Stir-fry for 2-3 minutes, stirring constantly.
3. Now, add meat chops and cook for 10 minutes.
4. Pour in the heavy cream and balsamic vinegar. Sprinkle with the remaining spices and give it a good stir. Bring it to a boil and cook for 10-15 more minutes, or until the sauce thickens.
5. Transfer to a serving dish and optionally, drizzle with some lemon juice before serving.
6. Enjoy!

Per Serving:
(Calories 464 | Total Fats 36.1g | Net Carbs: 2.5g | Protein 30.2g | Fiber: 0.2g)

Beef Cremini

(Total Time: 40 MIN | Serves: 4)

Ingredients:

- 1 lb beef shoulder roast, cut into bite-sized pieces
- 1 cup Cremini mushrooms, thinly sliced
- ½ cup heavy cream
- 1 small red onion, diced
- 1 tbsp butter
- 2 cups beef broth

Spices:
- 1 tsp salt
- 1 tsp dried thyme, ground
- ½ tsp white pepper, ground
- 1 tsp garlic powder

Directions:

1. Plug in the instant pot and press the "Sauté" button. Melt the butter in the stainless steel insert and add mushrooms. Sprinkle with salt and thyme. Cook for 10 minutes and then pour in the heavy cream. Bring it to a boil and simmer for 5 minutes, stirring occasionally.
2. When done, transfer the mushrooms along with liquid to a food processor. Pulse until creamy and smooth. Set aside.
3. Add the meat chops to the pot and sprinkle with white pepper, garlic powder, and a pinch of salt. Pour in the broth and securely lock the lid by moving the valve to the "Sealing" position. Set the timer for 15 minutes and cook on "High" pressure.
4. When done, perform a quick pressure release and open the pot.
5. Transfer the meat to a serving plate and drizzle with creamy sauce.
6. Serve immediately.

Per Serving:
(Calories 283 | Total Fats 17.2g | Net Carbs: 3.4g | Protein 26.7g | Fiber: 0.7g)

Beef Ragout

(Total Time: 40 MIN | Serves: 6)

Ingredients:

- 2 lbs beef steak, cut into bite-sized pieces
- 1 small onion, finely chopped
- 1 small celery stalk, chopped
- 1 small red chili pepper, diced
- 1 cup tomatoes, diced
- 4 garlic cloves, crushed
- 2 cups beef stock
- 1 tbsp olive oil

Spices:
- 1 tsp salt
- 1 tsp dried oregano, ground
- 1 tsp black pepper, ground
- 1 bay leaf

Directions:

1. Plug in the instant pot and grease the stainless steel insert with olive oil. Press the "Sauté" button and onions, celery, garlic, and chili pepper. Stir-fry for 4-5 minutes, or until the onions translucent.
2. Add meat chops and sprinkle with salt, oregano, and pepper. Pour in the beef stock and throw in the bay leaf. Securely lock the lid and adjust the steam release handle. Press the "Manual" button and set the timer for 20 minutes. Cook on "High" pressure. When you hear the cooker's end signal, perform a quick release of the pressure and open the lid.
3. Stir in the tomatoes and press the "Sauté" button. Bring it to a boil and cook for 10 more minutes, stirring occasionally. Remove the bay leaf and transfer all to a serving dish. Optionally, garnish with some finely chopped parsley or top with sour cream.

Per Serving:
(Calories 322 | Total Fats 12.1g | Net Carbs: 2.6g | Protein 47.4g | Fiber: 1g)

Beef & Lamb

Creamy Beef Chili

(Total Time: 30 MIN | Serves: 4)

Ingredients:

- 1 lb ground beef
- 2 cups tomatoes, diced
- 1 medium-sized red bell pepper, chopped
- 1 small red onion, chopped
- 3 garlic cloves, minced
- 1 tbsp olive oil
- 1 cup heavy cream
- ½ cup beef broth

Spices:
- ½ tsp chili powder
- 1 tsp kosher salt
- 1 tsp garlic powder
- ½ tsp smoked paprika
- ½ tsp dried rosemary, ground

Directions:

1. Plug in the instant pot and press the "Sauté" button. Grease the stainless steel insert with olive oil and add ground beef, onion, and bell pepper. Sprinkle with salt and garlic powder. Using a wooden spatula, stir well and cook for 5 minutes.
2. Add tomatoes and pour in the broth. Securely lock the lid and set the steam release handle. Press the "Manual" button and set the timer for 5 minutes. Cook on "High" pressure.
3. When done, perform a quick pressure release and open the pot. Stir in the heavy cream and sprinkle with chili powder, salt, paprika, and rosemary.
4. Press the "Sauté" button and cook for 10 more minutes.
5. Transfer all to a serving dish and enjoy!

Per Serving:
(Calories 390 | Total Fats 22.3g | Net Carbs: 7.7g | Protein 37.3g | Fiber: 2.3g)

Beef Brisket with Thyme Sauce

(Total Time: 45 MIN| Serves: 5)

Ingredients:

- 2 lbs beef brisket
- 1 cup heavy cream
- 1 cup beef stock
- 1 medium-sized onion, chopped
- 3 garlic cloves, finely chopped

Spices:
- 2 tsp fresh thyme, chopped
- 1 tsp sea salt
- ½ tsp black pepper, ground
- ½ tsp red pepper flakes

Directions:

1. Rinse the meat under cold running water and pat dry with a kitchen paper. Generously rub with salt and pepper and set aside.
2. Plug in your instant pot and add onions and garlic, press the "Sauté" button and cook for 3 minutes.
3. Now, add meat and pour in the beef stock and 1 cup of water. Securely lock the lid and adjust the steam release handle. Press the "Manual" button and set the timer for 25 minutes. Cook on "High" pressure.
4. When done, perform a quick pressure release and open the pot.
5. Stir in the heavy cream and the remaining spices. Simmer for 10 more minutes.
6. Enjoy!

Per Serving:
(Calories 437 | Total Fats 29.4g | Net Carbs: 3g | Protein 56.5g | Fiber: 0.8g)

Beef with Greens

(Total Time: 50 MIN | Serves: 8)

Ingredients:

- 2 lbs beef chuck roast, cut into bite-sized pieces
- 1 cup fresh spinach, chopped
- 1 cup fresh kale, chopped
- 1 small onion, chopped
- 4 garlic cloves, finely chopped
- 2 cups beef broth
- 2 tbsp butter

Spices:
- 1 tsp sea salt
- ½ tsp black pepper, ground
- ¼ tsp dried thyme, ground

Directions:

1. Combine spinach and kale in a large colander. Rinse thoroughly under cold running water and drain. Chop into small pieces and set aside.
2. Plug in the instant pot and press the "Sauté" button. Melt 1 tablespoon of the butter in the stainless steel insert and add garlic and onions. Cook for 3-4 minutes, stirring occasionally.
3. Add meat and sprinkle with salt and pepper. Pour in the broth and lock the lid. Set the steam release handle and press the "Manual" button. Set the timer for 20 minutes and cook on "High" pressure.
4. When done, perform a quick pressure release by moving the valve to the "Venting" position. Open the pot and add spinach, kale and the remaining butter. Cook for 5 more minutes, or until the greens are wilted.
5. Turn off the pot and transfer all to a serving bowl.
6. Optionally, top with sour cream or cream cheese and enjoy!

Per Serving:
(Calories 458 | Total Fats 34.8g | Net Carbs: 2.2g | Protein 31.5g | Fiber: 0.5g)

Quick Cheddar Beef Hash

(Total Time: 20 MIN | Serves: 4)

Ingredients:

- 1 lb ground beef
- 1 medium-sized green bell pepper, chopped
- 1 cup cauliflower, chopped
- 1 cup cheddar cheese
- 1 small celery stalk, chopped
- 1 tbsp fresh parsley, finely chopped
- 1 tbsp olive oil

Spices:
- ½ tsp black pepper, freshly ground
- ½ tsp smoked paprika, ground
- 1 tsp sea salt

Directions:

1. Plug the instant pot and press the "Sauté" button. Grease the stainless steel insert with olive oil. Add ground beef and cook for 5 minutes, or until lightly browned.
2. Now, add bell pepper, cauliflower, and parsley. Add about ¼ cup of water and continue to cook for another 5 minutes, or until vegetables are tender. Sprinkle all with smoked paprika, salt, and pepper.
3. Add the cheese on top and allow it to melt.
4. Turn off the pot and transfer all to a serving dish, using a large slotted spoon.
5. Optionally, top with sour cream and enjoy immediately.

Per Serving:
(Calories 373 | Total Fats 2.1g | Net Carbs: 3.1g | Protein 42.4g | Fiber: 1.3g)

Beef & Lamb

Mustard Cheese Meatballs

(Total Time: 20 MIN | Serves: 6)

Ingredients:

- 2 lbs lean ground beef
- 3 oz cheddar cheese
- 2 large eggs, beaten
- 2 garlic cloves, crushed
- 1 small Jalapeno pepper, chopped
- 1 tbsp butter
- 1 tbsp fresh parsley, finely chopped
- 1 tbsp Dijon mustard
- 1 cup beef stock

Spices:
- 1 tsp salt
- ¼ tsp smoked paprika, ground
- ½ tsp black pepper, ground

Directions:

1. In a large mixing bowl, combine ground beef, cheese, eggs, garlic, Jalapeno pepper, parsley, mustard, paprika, salt, and pepper.
2. Mix until well incorporated.
3. Shape the meatballs, about 1 to 1 1/2 –inch in diameter and set aside.
4. Plug in the instant pot and add butter to the stainless steel insert. Gently melt over the "Sauté" mode, stirring constantly.
5. Spread the meatballs on the bottom of the pot and slowly pour in the beef stock.
6. Securely lock the lid and set the steam release the handle by moving the valve to the "Sealing" position.
7. Press the "Manual" button and set the timer for 10 minutes. Cook on "High" pressure.
8. When done, perform a quick release of the pressure and open the pot.
9. Transfer the meatballs to a serving platter and drizzle with some of the liquid from the pot.
10. Optionally, garnish with some finely chopped cilantro before serving.

Per Serving:

(Calories 387 | Total Fats 17.9g | Net Carbs: 0.9g | Protein 52.2g | Fiber: 0.3g)

Chapter 7

Pork

Classic Meatloaf

(TotalTime: 70 MIN | Serves: 6)

Ingredients:

- 2 lbs ground pork
- 1 cup almond flour
- 2 small onions, finely chopped
- 2 spring onions, finely chopped
- ½ cup celery stalk, finely chopped
- 3 garlic cloves, crushed
- 2 tbsp butter
- 3 tbsp olive oil
- 1 cup cherry tomatoes, chopped

Spices:
- 1 tsp salt
- 2 tsp dried celery
- ½ tsp white pepper, ground

Directions:

1. In a large bowl, combine the ground pork with onions, spring onions, celery stalk, and garlic. Sprinkle with salt, celery, and pepper.
2. Now add about one cup of almond flour and mix well agan. Optionally, add a handful of finely chopped almonds for a crunchy taste.
3. Transfer the mixture to a large piece of plastic foil and wrap tightly. Refrigerate for 30 minutes.
4. Meanwhile, place cherry tomatoes in a food processor and process until smooth. Add olive oil and mix well. Set aisde.
5. Remove the meat from the refrigerator and place back in the mixing bowl. Add tomatoes and butter. Mix well again and shape the meatloaf using a large piece of plastic foil. Place in a baking dish and loosely cover with aluminum foil.
6. Plug in the instant pot and set the trivet at the bottom of the inner pot. Pour in one cup of water and place the baking dish on top.
7. Seal the lid and set the steam release handle to the "Sealing" position. Press the "Manual" button and set the timer for 20 minutes on high pressure.
8. When done, perform a quick pressure release and open the lid. Remove the pan from the pot and chill for a while.
9. Serve and enjoy!

Per Serving:
(Calories 358 | Total Fats: 18.5g | Net Carbs: 3.8g | Protein: 41.4g | Fiber: 1.7g)

Spicy Burgers

(TotalTime: 15 MIN | Serves: 6)

Ingredients:

- 1 lb ground pork
- 2 onions
- 1 red chili pepper
- ½ cup fresh parsley, finely chopped
- 3 tbsp almond flour

Spices:
- ½ tsp salt
- ¼ tsp garlic powder
- ¼ tsp black pepper, freshly ground

Directions:

1. Place the onions and chili pepper in a food processor and process for 30 seconds. Transfer to a bowl and add the meat. Sprinkle with parsley, almond flour, and spices.
2. Mix well and shape burgers, about 2-inch in diameter.
3. Place burgers in the steam basket and pour in one cup of water in the inner pot.
4. Seal the lid and set the steam release handle to the "Sealing" position. Press the "Manual" button and set the timer for 7 minutes on high pressure.
5. When done, perform a quick pressure release and open the lid.
6. Remove burgers from the pot and serve immediately.

Per Serving:
(Calories 198 | Total Fats: 4.9g | Net Carbs: 4.4g | Protein: 30.9g | Fiber: 1.7g)

Garlic Pork Chops

(TotalTime: 25 MIN | Serves: 4)

Ingredients:

- 2 pork chops, 1-inch thick
- 1 cup onions, finely chopped
- 3 garlic cloves, crushed
- 4 bacon slices, chopped
- 2 tbsp oil

Spices:
- 1 tsp salt
- 1 tsp black pepper, ground
- ¼ tsp garlic powder
- ½ tsp dried thyme

Directions:

1. Plug in the instant pot and press the "Saute" button. Grease the inner pot with oil and heat up.
2. Rub the meat with salt, pepper, garlic and thyme. Set aside.
3. Add onions and garlic to the pot. Sauté for 2-3 minutes and then add the bacon. Continue to cook for another 2 minutes, stirring constantly.
4. Now add the seasoned meat and briefly brown for 2 minutes on each side.
5. Press the "Cancel" button and pour in one cup of water. Seal the lid and set the steam release handle to the "Sealing" position.
6. Press the "Manual" button and set the timer for 13 minutes.
7. When done, release the pressure naturally and open the lid.
8. Optionally, brown the meat in a large non-stick skillet over medium-high heat before serving.

Per Serving:
(Calories 340 | Total Fats: 18.8g | Net Carbs: 3g | Protein: 37.2g | Fiber: 0.7g)

Pork

Pork Steak in Mushroom Sauce

(TotalTime: 30 MIN| Serves: 4)

Ingredients:

- 4 pork steaks (about 8oz each)
- 1 cup button mushrooms, sliced
- ¼ cup apple cider vinegar
- 3 tbsp butter
- 2 cups heavy cream
- ¼ cup cottage cheese
- ¼ cup crumbled feta cheese
- 3 tbsp Parmesan, grated
- 4 cups beef broth
- 1 small onion, roughly chopped
- 1 celery stalk, chopped
- ½ cup celery leaves, whole

Spices:
- 2 tsp salt
- 1 tbsp peppercorn
- 2 bay leaves
- 1 thyme sprig, fresh

Directions:

1. Rinse the meat under cold running water and place at the bottom of the instant pot. Pour in the broth and apple cider. Add salt, peppercorn, by leaves, thyme sprig, onion, celery stalk, and celery leaves. Seal the lid and set the steam release handle.
2. Press the "Meat" button and cook for 15 minutes.
3. When done, perform a quick pressure release and open the lid. Remove the meat along with the broth from the pot and set aisde.
4. Now press the "Saute" button and grease the inner pot with butter. Add pre-cooked onions from the broth and give it a good stir. Season with salt and add mushrooms.
5. Cook for 5-6 minutes and then add the cheese and heavy cream. Give it a good stir and remove from the pot.
6. Drizzle over the meat and serve.

Per Serving:
(Calories 721 | Total Fats: 44g | Net Carbs: 5.6g | Protein: 71.8g |Fiber: 0.6g)

Rosemary Pork Shoulder

(TotalTime: 40 MIN | Serves: 4)

Ingredients:

- 2lbs pork shoulder roast
- 2 shallots, sliced
- 4 garlic cloves, crushed
- 3 tbsp olive oil
- 3 tbsp Dijon mustard

Spices:
- 1 tsp salt
- 1 tbsp fresh rosemary, finely chopped
- ½ tsp white pepper, freshly ground

Directions:

1. Rinse well the meat and sprinkle with salt and pepper. Set aside.
2. Take a round oven-safe bowl and coat with olive oil. Make a layer with shallots and sprinkle with garlic and fresh rosemary.
3. Place the meat on top and generously brush with Dijon mustard. Loosely cover with aluminum foil and set aside.
4. Plug in the instant pot and set the trivet in the inner pot. Pour in one cup of water and place the bowl on the trivet.
5. Seal the lid and set the steam release handle to the "Sealing" position and press the "Manual" button.
6. Set the timer for 25 minutes on high pressure.
7. When done, release the pressure naturally and open the lid. Remove the bowl from the pot and chill for a while.
8. Serve immediately.

Per Serving:
(Calories 430 | Total Fats: 19g | Net Carbs: 2g | Protein: 60.2g | Fiber: 0.5g)

Balsamic Chops with Onions

(TotalTime: 55 MIN| Serves: 4)

Ingredients:

- 4 pork chops, about 1-inch thick
- 2 large onions, chopped
- 4 garlic cloves, whole
- 3 tbsp balsamic vinegar
- 3 tbsp butter
- 2 tbsp olive oil

Spices:
- 1 tsp salt
- 1 tsp dried thyme

Directions:

1. Rub the meat with spices and set aside.
2. Grease a fitting baking pan with oil and place chops along with oinions and whole garlic cloves. Drizzle with some more oil and tightly wrap with aluminum foil.
3. Plug in the instant pot andpour in two cups of water. Set the trivet at the bottom of the inner pot and place the pan on top.
4. Seal the lid and set the steam release handle. Press the "Manual" button and cook for 35 minutes on high pressure.
5. When done, perform a quick pressure release. Carefully open the lid and remve the baking pan with pork.
6. Remove the trivet and the remaining water from the pot and press the "Saute" button.
7. Grease the inner pot with butter and heat up. Add balsamic vinegar and briefly cook – for 1 minute.
8. Now add onions from the baking pan and give it a good stir. Cook for anoher minute and finally add the meat.
9. Brown for 2-3 minute on each side.
10. When done, remove from the pot and serve immediately.

Per Serving:
(Calories 429 | Total Fats: 35.6g | Net Carbs: 6.4g | Protein: 19.1g |Fiber: 1.7g)

Sweet Pork with Cauliflower

(Total Time: 45 MIN | Serves: 4)

Ingredients:

- 2 lbs pork shoulder, cut into bite-sized pieces
- 2 cups cauliflower, cut into florets
- 5 bacon slices, chopped
- 2 celery stalks, chopped
- 1 small onion, finely chopped
- 4 tbsp olive oil
- 4 cups beef broth

Spices:
- 1 ½ tsp salt
- 2 tsp peppercorn
- ¼ cup stevia crystal
- 1 tsp onion powder
- ½ tsp garlic powder

Directions:

1. Grease the bottom of the instant pot with oil and make the first layer with meat. Season with some salt and then add onions and celery stalks. Optionally, sprinkle with some more salt and add cauliflower. Top with bacon and gently pour in the broth.
2. Seal the lid and set the steam release handle to the "Sealing" position. Press the "Manual" button and set the timer for 15 mninutes on high pressure.
3. When done, release the pressure naturally and open the lid. Remove the meat and vegetables from the pot but keep the broth.
4. Now press the "Saute" button and add stevia crystal, some more salt, peppercorn, onion powder, and garlic powder.
5. Gently simmer until the liquid has reduced in half.
6. Remove the peppercorn from the pot and add the meat. Coat well with the sauce and serve with cauliflower.
7. Drizzle with some more sweet sauce before serving.

Per Serving:
(Calories 647 | Total Fats: 49.2g | Net Carbs: 2.7g | Protein: 45.1g | Fiber: 1.2g)

Pork Chops with Sauteed Peppers

 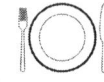

(TotalTime: 35 MIN| Serves: 5)

Ingredients:

- 1 lb pork chops, cut into bite-sized pieces
- 2 red bell peppers, sliced
- 2 chili peppers, chopped
- 2 small onions, finely chopped
- 2 bacon slices, chopped
- 2 tbsp butter, unsalted
- 1 cup beef broth

Spices:
- 2 tsp Italian seasoning
- ¼ tsp salt

Directions:

1. Rinse the meat under cold running water and sprinkle with one teaspoon of Italian seasoning. Place in the instant pot and pour in the broth.
2. Seal the lid and set the steam release handle. Press the "Manual" button and set the timer for 10 minutes on high pressure.
3. When done, release the pressure by moving the handle to the "Venting" position and carefully open the lid.
4. Remove the meat from the pot along with the broh and press the "Saute" button.
5. Grease the inner pot with butter and add onion. Sauté for 2 minutes and then add peppers. Sprinkle with salt and the remaining Italian seasoning and cook for 2-3 minutes.
6. Now add bacon and stir well. Optionally, add some more salt or Italian seasoning and cook for 5 minutes. If necessary, add some beef broth – about 2 tablespoons at the time.
7. Finally, add the meat and give it a good stir. Cook for 5 minutes.
8. Press the "Cancel" button and serve immediately.

Per Serving:
(Calories 407| Total Fats: 30.8g | Net Carbs: 5.4g | Protein: 25g |Fiber: 1.3g)

Pork Shoulder with Sweet Potatoes

(Total Time: 30 MIN | Serves: 5)

Ingredients:

- 2 lbs pork shoulder, cut into bite-sized pieces
- 1 large sweet potato, chopped into bite-sized chunks
- 1 cup purple cabbage, shredded
- 1 cup cauliflower, chopped into florets
- 2 chili peppers, sliced
- 4 garlic cloves, whole
- 1 celery stalk, chopped
- 4 tbsp butter

Spices:
- 2 tsp salt
- 1 tsp white pepper, freshly ground
- 2 bay leaves, whole
- 1 tsp dried thyme

Directions:

1. Place the meat in the pot and pour in enough water to cover. Seal the lid and set the steam release handle. Press the "Meat" button.
2. When done, perform a quick pressure release and open the lid.
3. Now add the remaining ingredients and optionally pour in one more cup of water. Stir well and season with salt, pepper, thyme, and bay leaves.
4. Seal the lid again and set the steam release handle to the "Sealing" position. Press the "Manual" button and set the timer for 7 minutes on high pressure.
5. When you hear the cooker's end singnal, release the pressure naturally for 10-15 minutes and then carefully open the lid.
6. Serve immediately.

Per Serving:
(Calories 657| Total Fats: 48.1g | Net Carbs: 8.2g | Protein: 43.8g |Fiber: 2.2g)

Sweet Garlic Pork

(TotalTime: 45 MIN| Serves: 6)

Ingredients:

- 2 lbs pork chops
- ½ cup celery stalks, chopped
- 2 large onions, finely chopped
- 4 garlic cloves
- 1 cup cherry tomatoes
- ¼ cup soy sauce
- 3 tbsp butter
- 3 tbsp apple cider vinegar

Spices:
- 1 tsp salt
- 2 tbsp stevia crystal
- ½ tsp ginger powder
- ½ tsp chili flakes

Directions:

1. Rinse well the meat and pat dry each piece with some kitchen paper. Place on a large cutting board and remove the bones. Chop into bite-sized pieces and place in a deep bowl. Sprinkle with salt, ginger, and chili flakes. Drizzle with soy sauce and set aside.
2. Plug in the instant pot and press the "Saute" button. Grease the inner pot with butter and heat up. Add onions, garlic, and celery stalks. Cook for 3-4 minutes, stirring constantly. Now add cherry tomatoes and sprinkle with stevia. Continue to cook for 5 minutes or until soft.
3. Finally, add the meat and drizzle with apple cider vinegar. Stir fry for another 4-5 minutes and then pour in one cup of water.
4. Press the "Cancel" button and seal the lid. Set the steam release handle to the "Sealing" position and press the "Manual" button.
5. Set the timer for 10 minutes on high pressure. when done, release the pressure naturally and open the lid.
6. Optionally, sprinkle with freshly chopped parsley and serve immediately.

Per Serving:
(Calories 569| Total Fats: 43.5g | Net Carbs: 5.3g | Protein: 35.6g |Fiber: 1.7g)

Pork Loin with Leeks

(TotalTime: 45 MIN | Serves: 4)

Ingredients:

- 1 lb pork loin, boneless
- 1 onion, finely chopped
- 2 large leeks, chopped
- ¼ cup apple cider vinegar
- 2 cups beef broth
- 1 celery stalk, chopped
- 4 tbsp olive oil

Spices:
- 1 ½ tsp sea salt
- 2 tbsp stevia crystal (or powder)
- 2 tsp dried celery
- ¼ tsp dried thyme
- ¼ tsp chili powder

Directions:

1. Rub the meat with salt and place in the pot. Pour in enough water to cover and seal the lid.
2. Set the steam release handle and press the "Maual" button. Set the timer for 25 minutes on high pressure.
3. When done, perform a quick pressure release and open the lid. Transfer the meat to a bowl and remove the water. Set aside.
4. Press the "Saute" button and heat up the oil. Add onions, leeks, and celery. Give it a good stir and cook for 3-4 minutes.
5. Meanwhile, place the meat on a cutting board and chop into bite-sized pieces. Add to the pot and stir well. Drizzle with apple cider vinegar and season with spices.
6. Brown for 4-5 minutes, stirring occasionally.
7. Press the "Cancel" button and serve immediately.

Per Serving:
(Calories 456 | Total Fats: 30.6g | Net Carbs: 8.1g | Protein: 34.4g | Fiber: 1.5g)

Easy Pork Ribs

(TotalTime: 30 MIN | Serves: 5)

Ingredients:

- 2 lbs pork ribs
- 1 cup cauliflower, chopped into florets
- 2 celery stalks, chopped
- 2 red bell peppers, chopped
- ½ cup onions, finely chopped
- 1 cup portobello mushrooms, chopped
- 1 cup tomatoes, diced
- 2 tbsp hot chili sauce, sugar-free
- 2 garlic cloves, whole
- 1 tsp apple cider vinegar
- 3 tbsp butter
- 5 cups beef broth

Spices:
- 2 tsp salt
- ½ tsp black pepper, freshly ground
- 1 tsp dried celery
- 2 tsp onion powder

Directions:

1. Place the ribs in the pot and pour in enough water to cover. Add celery stalks and seal the lid. Set the steam release handle to the "Sealing" position and press the "Meat" button.
2. Set the timer for 15 minutes on high pressure.
3. When done, perform a quick pressure release and open the lid.
4. Now stir in the remaining ingredients and sprinkle with salt, pepper, celery, and onion powder. Stir all well and seal the lid again.
5. Set the steam release handle to the "Sealing" position and continue to cook for another 7 minutes.
6. When done, perform a quick pressure release and open the lid.
7. Serve immediately.

Per Serving:
(Calories 633 | Total Fats: 40.7g | Net Carbs: 7.1g | Protein: 54.9g | Fiber: 2.1g)

Italian Roast

(TotalTime: 45 MIN | Serves: 4)

Ingredients:

- 1 lb boneless pork loin, chopped into 4 pieces
- 1 cup olive oil
- ¼ cup apple cider vinegar
- 2 tbsp Dijon mustard
- 1 lemon, sliced
- 3 tbsp butter

Spices:
- 1 tbsp dried rosemary
- 2 tsp garlic powder
- 2 tsp smoked paprika
- ½ tsp dried thyme
- 2 tsp salt
- 1 tsp white pepper, freshly ground

Directions:

1. In a medium-sized bowl, combine together olive oil, apple cider, Dijon, lemon slices, dried rosemary, garlic powder, smoked paprika, thyme, salt, and pepper. Mix well and add pork.
2. Coat each piece with the mixture and place in a large Ziploc bag, refrigerate overnight.
3. Plug in the instant pot and pour in one cup of water. Set the trivet at the bottom of the stainless steel insert.
4. Remove the meat from the refrigerator about 30 minutes before cooking. Place in an oven-safe bowl and drizzle with some of the marinade – about 3 tablespoons.
5. Loosely cover with aluminum foil and seal the lid. Set the steam release handle to the "Sealing" position and press the "Meat" button. Cook for 20 minutes.
6. When done, release the pressure naturally and open the lid.
7. Preheat the oven to 400 degrees. Line some parchment paper over a baking sheet and add the meat.
8. Generously brush with the marinade and roast for 15 minutes.
9. When done, remove from the oven and brush with butter. Serve immediately.

Per Serving:

(Calories 351| Total Fats: 25.4g | Net Carbs: 0.2g | Protein: 29.9g |Fiber: 0.1g)

Pork

Chinese Pork Strips

(TotalTime: 55 MIN| Serves: 4)

Ingredients:

- 1 lb pork neck, cut into 2-inch long strips
- ½ cup canned bamboo, chopped
- 1 spring onion, finely chopped
- 1 egg
- 3 tbsp vegetable oil
- 2 red bell peppers, sliced into strips
- 2 tbsp dark soy sauce
- 2 tbsp light soy sauce
- 1 tbsp rice vinegar

Spices:
- ½ tsp salt
- ½ tsp stevia powder

Directions:

1. Rinse the meat and place on a large cutting board. Using a sharp knife, cut into strips and place in a deep bowl. Add one egg, salt, and soy sauce. Cover with a lid and set it sit for 10-15 minutes.
2. Plug in the instant pot and press the "Saute" button. Add half of the meat and cook for 6-7 minutes, stirring constantly. Repeat with the remaining meat and remove from the pot. Set aside.
3. Now, grease the inner pot with oil and heat up. Add bamboo and sliced bell peppers. Cook for 7-8 minutes, stirring constantly.
4. Sprinkle with stevia and rice vinegar and add the meat. Give it a good stir and add onions.
5. Continue to cook for another 2-3 minutes.
6. Press the "Cancel" button and serve immediately.

Per Serving:
(Calories 302 | Total Fats: 15.5g | Net Carbs: 5.3g | Protein: 33g |Fiber: 1.3g)

Simple Tomato Pork Chops

(Total Time: 40 MIN | Serves: 2)

Ingredients:

- 2 pork chops, with bones
- 1 cup cherry tomatoes
- 1 green bell pepper, sliced
- 1 small onion, finely chopped
- 4 tbsp olive oil
- 1 cup beef broth

Spices:
- ½ tsp salt
- ½ tsp white pepper, freshly ground
- ¼ tsp garlic powder

Directions:

1. Place the meat in the pot and season with salt. Pour in the broth and seal the lid. Set the steam release handle to the "Sealing" position and press the "Manual" button.
2. Set the timer for 15 minutes on high pressure. When done, release the pressure naturally and open the lid.
3. Remove the meat from the pot and transfer to a deep bowl. Set aside.
4. Now, press the "Saute" button and grease the inner pot with olive oil. Heat up and add onions and peppers. Sprinkle with some more salt. Cook for 5-6 minutes and then add cherry tomatoes. Pour in about ¼ cup of the broth and simmer for 10-12 minutes, stirring occasionally.
5. Season with pepper and garlic powder. Optionally, add some red pepper flakes. Transfer the mixture to a food processor and process until smooth. Drizzle over pork chope and serve immediately.

Per Serving:
(Calories 633| Total Fats: 37g | Net Carbs: 9.1g | Protein: 63.6g |Fiber: 2.6g)

Sweet Coconut Pork

(TotalTime: 1 HOUR | Serves: 6)

Ingredients:

- 4 pork chops, with bones
- 1 large onion, finely chopped
- 1 chili pepper, finely chopped
- 1 cup heavy cream
- ¼ cup coconut milk
- 2 tbsp coconut cream
- 3 tbsp almond flour
- 2 tbsp butter
- 1 cup cauliflower, chopped into florets

Spices:
- 1 tsp salt
- ½ tsp white pepper, freshly ground
- 2 tsp stevia powder
- 1 tsp rum extract

Directions:

1. In a medium-sized bowl, combine heavy cream, coconut milk, coconut cream, salt, pepper, stevia, and rum. Add the meat and coat well with the mixture. Transfer to a large Ziploc bag. Seal the bag and refrigerate overnight.
2. Plug in the instant pot and set the trivet at the bottom of the inner pot. Remove the pork from the refrigerator and place in a deep oven-safe bowl along with the marinade.
3. Place the bowl in the pot and pour in about one cup of water in the inner pot. Seal the lid and set the steam release handle to the "Sealing" posisiton.
4. Press the "Manual" button and set the timer for 20 minutes on high pressure.
5. When done, perform a quick pressure release and open the lid. Remove the bowl with the pork and press the "Saute" button.
6. Grease the inner pot with butter and heat up. Add onions, peppers, and cauliflower. Stir well and cook for 6-7 minutes.
7. Now add the pork along with its sauce and stir in almond flour. Continue to cook for another 3-4 minutes, coating the meat well with the sauce.
8. Press the "Cancel" button and serve immediately.

Per Serving:
(Calories 462| Total Fats: 24.6g | Net Carbs: 7.9g | Protein: 49.4g |Fiber: 1.6g)

Button Mushroom and Pepper Pork

(TotalTime: 40 MIN| Serves: 4)

Ingredients:

- 1 lb pork loin, cut into bite-sized pieces
- 2 red bell peppers, sliced
- 1 cup button mushrooms, sliced
- 1 garlic clove, crushed
- ½ cup sun-dried tomatoes
- 3 tbsp olive oil
- 2 cups beef broth

Spices:
- ½ tsp salt
- ½ tsp dried oregano
- ¼ tsp black pepper, freshly ground

Directions:

1. Rinse the meat and place on a cutting board. Chop into bite-sized pieces and set aside.
2. Plug in the instant pot and press the "Saute" button. Grease the inner pot with oil and heat up. Add peppers and garlic. Cook for 4-5 minutes and then add the pork.
3. Brown on all sides for a couple of minutes, stirring constantly.
4. Now season with salt, pepper, and oregano. Add mushrooms, tomatoes, and pour in the broth. Stir well and seal the lid.
5. Set the steam release handle to the "Sealing" position and press the "Manual" button.
6. Set the timer for 15 minutes on high pressure.
7. When done, release the pressure naturally for 15-20 minutes before serving.

Per Serving:
(Calories 299| Total Fats: 15.4g | Net Carbs: 5.4g | Protein: 33.5g |Fiber: 1.3g)

Pork Neck with Sesame Seeds and Soy Sauce

(TotalTime: 45 MIN| Serves: 4)

Ingredients:

- 1 lb pork neck, chopped into bite-sized pieces
- 1 large onion, finely chopped
- 4 garlic cloves, whole
- ½ cup canned tomatoes, sugar-free
- ½ cup dark soy sauce
- 3 tbsp sesame seeds
- 3 tbsp oil

Spices:
- 1 tsp salt
- 2 tsp stevia powder
- ½ tsp ginger powder

Directions:

1. Plug in the instant pot and press the "Saute" button. Grease the inner pot with oil and heat up. Add onions and cook until translucent.
2. Now add garlic and chopped meat. Pour in about ¼ cup of water and cook for 20 minutes, stirring occasionally.
3. Finally, add tomatoes, soy sauce, and sesame seeds. Season with salt, ginger powder, and stevia powder. Give it a good stir and continue to cook for 10 minutes.
4. Press the "Cancel" button and serve immediately. Optionally, sprinkle with some freshly chopped parsley or spring onions.

Per Serving:
(Calories 328| Total Fats: 17.6g | Net Carbs: 8.3g | Protein: 31.8g |Fiber: 1.9g)

Apple Cider Pork Ribs

(Total Time: 55 MIN | Serves: 5)

Ingredients:

- 2 lbs pork ribs, cut into smaller pieces
- 2 green bell peppers, sliced
- 2 celery stalks, chopped
- ¼ cup celery leaves, chopped
- 1 onion, finely chopped
- 2 eggs, whole
- ¼ cup light soy sauce
- 3 tbsp apple cider vinegar
- ¼ cup canned tomatoes, sugar-free
- 1 cup beef broth

Spices:
- ¼ cup swerve
- 2 tsp salt
- 1 tsp chili powder

Directions:

1. Place ribs in the pot and pour in enough water to cover. Seal the lid and set the steam release handle to the "Sealing" position. Press the "Meat" button and set the timer for 20 minutes on high pressure
2. When done, perform a quick release and open the lid. Transfer the ribs to a deep bowl and chill for a while.
3. Remove the water press the "Saute" button.
4. Now, whisk together eggs, apple cider, soy sauce, swerve, salt, and chili powder. Rub the meat with this mixture and let it sit for a while.
5. Add celery stalks, onions, and peppers to the pot and cook for 8-10 minutes, stirring constantly. Season with some more salt and add tomatoes. Pour in the broth and continue to cook until most of the liquid has evaporated.
6. Now add the prepared pork and coat well with vegetables.
7. Press the "Cancel" button and sprinkle with fresh celery leaves. Let it sit for a while before serving.

Per Serving:
(Calories 321| Total Fats: 8.6g | Net Carbs: 6.1g | Protein: 51.7g | Fiber: 1.3g)

Zucchini Pork

(TotalTime: 1 HOUR| Serves: 4)

Ingredients:

- 1 lb pork neck, chopped into bite-sized pieces
- 2 red bell peppers, chopped
- 1 large tomato, roughly chopped
- 1 cup cauliflower florets
- 1 zucchini, spiralized into noodles
- 1 small onion, finely chopped
- 2 garlic cloves, crushed
- 1 cup button mushrooms, sliced
- 2 tbsp apple cider vinegar
- 2 tbsp butter
- 2 tbsp soy sauce
- 1 egg white

Spices:
- 1 tsp salt
- 2 bay leaves
- 2 tbsp stevia powder
- 1 tbsp cayenne pepper
- ½ tsp ginger powder

Directions:

1. In a small bowl, combine egg whites, soy sauce, apple cider, salt, stevia, half of the cayenne pepper, and ginger powder.
2. Generously brush the meat with this mixture and let it sit for 15-20 minutes.
3. Plug in the instant pot and add butter. Heat up and add the meat. Cook for 4-5 minutes, stirring constantly.
4. Remove the meat from the pot and add onions, garlic, mushrooms, peppers, tomato, and cauliflower.
5. Continue to cook for 10-12 minutes.
6. Finally, add the meat, bay leaf, and pour in 1 cup of water. Seal the lid and set the steam release handle to the "Sealing" posisiton.
7. Press the "Manual" button and set the timer for 13 minutes on high pressure.
8. When done, perform a quick pressure release and open the lid. Stir in zuccnhini noodles and press the "Saute" button.
9. Cook for 7-8 minutes, stirring occasionally.
10. Serve with grated Parmesan cheese or freshly chopped parsley.

Per Serving:
(Calories 277| Total Fats: 10.2g | Net Carbs: 9.5g | Protein: 34.1g |Fiber: 3.2g)

Steamed Pork Neck

(TotalTime: 40 MIN | Serves: 3)

Ingredients:

- 1 lb pork neck, cut into 3 pieces
- 3 garlic cloves, crushed
- 2 cups cauliflower florets
- 3 tbsp apple cider vinegar
- 4 tbsp olive oil

Spices:
- 2 tsp sea salt
- 1 tsp white pepper, freshly ground
- 1 tbsp cayenne pepper
- 1 tbsp dried celery

Directions:

1. Rinse the meat under cold running water and place on a cutting board. Using a sharp cutting knife, cut into 3 equal pieces. Rub each piece with salt, white pepper, cayenne pepper, and celery. Set aside.
2. Grease a small round baking pan with oil and add cauliflower. Top with pork and sprinkle with apple cider vinegar.
3. Plug in the instant pot and position a trivet at the bottom of the inner pot. Place the baking pan on the trivet and pour in 2 cups of water in the inner pot.
4. Seal the lid and set the steam release handle to the "Sealing" position. Press the "Manual" button and set the timer for 25 minutes on high pressure.
5. When done, perform a quick pressure release and open the lid.
6. Remove the baking pan from the pot and chill for a while. Serve with some Greek yogurt or cottage cheese.

Per Serving:
(Calories 401| Total Fats: 24.1g | Net Carbs: 3g | Protein: 41.1g | Fiber: 1.7g)

Portobello Pork Butt

(TotalTime: 1 HOUR | Serves: 4)

Ingredients:

- 1 lb pork butt
- 2 garlic cloves, crushed
- 1 cup Portobello mushrooms, sliced
- ½ cup dried shiitake
- 4 tbsp soy sauce
- 3 tbsp oil
- 2 tbsp apple cider vinegar

Spices:
- 2 tsp stevia powder
- 1 tsp salt
- 1 tsp turmeric powder

Directions:

1. Place the meat on a cutting board and cut 2-inch long strips. Set aside.
2. Place shiitake in a bowl and pour in enough water to cover. Soak for 10-15 minutes. Drain and set aside.
3. Plug in the instant pot and heat the oil. Add the meat and season with salt, turmeric, and stevia. Stir well and cook for 10 minutes.
4. Stir in Portobello mushrooms, soaked shiitake, and garlic. Continue to cook for 7-8 minutes, stirring constantly.
5. Finally, pour in the soy sauce and give it a good stir. Continue to cook for another 5 minutes. If necessary, add about 2-3 tablespoons of water.
6. Press the "Cancel" button and serve immediately.

Per Serving:
(Calories 545 | Total Fats: 28.4g | Net Carbs: 6.1g | Protein: 62.4g | Fiber: 0.8g)

Pork Chops with Cheese and Prosciutto

(Total Time: 55 MIN | Serves: 5)

Ingredients:

- 5 pork chops, boneless
- ½ cup cottage cheese
- 3 oz prosciutto
- 2 tbsp balsamic vinegar
- 1 onion, finely chopped
- 2 garlic cloves, crushed
- 4 tbsp olive oil
- ½ cup diced canned tomatoes, sugar-free

Spices:
- 1 tsp salt
- ½ tsp black pepper, freshly ground
- 1 tsp dried basil

Directions:

1. Rinse well the meat and pat dry with a kitchen towel. Place on a cutting board and remove the bones. Rub well with some olive oil, salt, pepper, and basil. Let it sit for 15 minutes.
2. Plug in the instant pot and position a trivet at the bottom of the inner pot. Pour in one cup of water and set aside.
3. Transfer the meat into a small baking pan. Drizzle with some more olive oil and add cheese and prosciutto. Loosely cover with aluminum foil and place in the pot.
4. Press the "Manual" button and set the steam release handle. Set the timer for 20 minutes on high pressure.
5. When done, perform a quick pressure release and open the lid. Remove the pan and set aside.
6. Now press the "Saute" button and grease the inner pot with some oil. Add onions and cook until translucent. Pour in tomatoes and cook for 10-12 minutes, stirring occasionally. Optionally, season with some more salt or dried basil.
7. Remove from the pot and drizzle over meat. Serve immediately.

Per Serving:
(Calories 416 | Total Fats: 19g | Net Carbs: 3.6g | Protein: 54.6g | Fiber: 0.7g)

Chapter 8
Vegetables and Vegetarian Dishes

Cauliflower Broccoli Stir-Fry

(Total Time: 20 MIN | Serves: 3)

Ingredients:

- 2 cups cauliflower, chopped
- 1 cup broccoli, chopped
- 3 garlic cloves, finely chopped
- 1 tbsp olive oil
- 2 eggs

Spices:
- ½ tsp salt
- ¼ tsp black pepper, ground
- ¼ tsp red pepper flakes
- ¼ tsp onion powder

Directions:

1. Plug in the instant pot and grease the stainless steel insert with olive oil. Press the "Saute" button and add garlic. Stir-fry for 2 minutes and add cauliflower and broccoli. Sprinkle with salt, pepper, red pepper flakes, and onion powder.
2. Stir and cook for 5 minutes.
3. Now, add about ¼ cup of water and cook for 5 more minutes, stirring occasionally.
4. Poach the egg on top and season with some more salt. Cook for 2-3 minutes more and turn off the pot.
5. Using a large spatula, transfer all to a serving plate.
6. Optionally, top with sour cream or some Greek yogurt.

Per Serving:
(Calories 115 | Total Fats 7.8g | Net Carbs: 4.3g | Protein 6.1g | Fiber: 2.8g)

Spinach Celery Stew

(Total Time: 15 MIN | Serves: 4)

Ingredients:

- 2 cups fresh spinach, chopped
- 1 cup celery leaves, chopped
- 1 cup celery stalks, chopped
- 2 garlic cloves, minced
- 1 small onion, chopped
- 2 cups heavy cream
- 1 tbsp lemon juice
- 2 tbsp butter

Spices:
- 1 tbsp fresh mint, torn
- 1 tsp salt
- ½ tsp black pepper, ground

Directions:

1. In a large colander, combine spinach and celery. Rinse well under running water and drain. Transfer to a cutting board cut into bite-sized pieces. Set aside.
2. Plug in your instant pot and press the " Saute" button. Add butter and stir constantly until melts.
3. Add celery stalks, garlic, and onions. Cook for 2 minutes and add celery leaves and spinach. Sprinkle with salt and pepper. Cook for 2-3 minutes and pour in the heavy cream.
4. Securely lock the lid and press the "Manual" button. Adjust the steam release handle and set the timer for 5 minutes. Cook on "High" pressure.
5. When you hear the cooker's end signal, perform a quick release of the pressure and open the pot.
6. Stir in the mint and lemon juice. Let it chill for 5 minutes before serving.
7. Enjoy!

Per Serving:
(Calories 278 | Total Fats 28.2g | Net Carbs: 4.3g | Protein 2.3g | Fiber: 1.4g)

Vegetables and Vegetarian Dishes

Creamy Collard Greens

(Total Time: 25 MIN| Serves: 4)

Ingredients:

- 1 lb collard greens, chopped
- ½ cup bacon, cut into bite-sized pieces
- 1 medium-sized onion, chopped
- 1 cup sour cream
- ½ tsp balsamic vinegar
- 1 tbsp olive oil
- 2 garlic cloves, finely chopped

Spices:
- 1 tsp red pepper flakes
- 1 tsp sea salt
- ¼ tsp black pepper, ground
- ½ tsp Italian seasoning

Directions:

1. Plug in your instant pot and add the bacon to the stainless steel insert. Press the "Saute" button and cook for 3-4 minutes, or until crisp. Remove the bacon from the pot and add olive oil. When hot, add onions and garlic. Stir-fry for 3-4 minutes, or until the onions translucent.
2. Add collard greens and cook for 2 minutes. Sprinkle with salt, pepper, Italian seasoning, and red pepper flakes. Pour in 1 cup of water and securely lock the lid. Adjust the steam release handle and press the "Manual" button. Set the timer for 5 minutes and cook on "High" pressure.
3. When done, perform a quick pressure release and open the pot.
4. Stir in the sour cream, balsamic vinegar, and bacon. Press the "Saute" button and cook for 2-3 minutes more, or until heated through.
5. Turn off the pot and transfer all to a serving plate.
6. Enjoy!

Per Serving:
(Calories 214 | Total Fats 17.6g | Net Carbs: 7.7g | Protein 5.7g | Fiber: 17.6g)

Vegetables and Vegetarian Dishes

Asparagus in Garlic Sauce

(Total Time: 20 MIN | Serves: 4)

Ingredients:

- 2 lbs asparagus, trimmed and cut into bite-sized pieces
- 1 cup heavy cream
- 5 garlic cloves, peeled
- 1 tbsp apple cider vinegar
- 1 tbsp fresh parsley, finely chopped
- 1 small onion, peeled and quartered
- 2 tbsp butter
- 1 tbsp olive oil

Spices:
- ½ tsp dried thyme, ground
- ¼ tsp dried oregano, ground
- 1 tsp salt
- ½ tsp black pepper, ground

Directions:

1. Rinse the asparagus and trim off the woody ends. Cut into bite-sized pieces and set aside.
2. In a food processor, combine heavy cream, garlic, apple cider vinegar, parsley, onion, olive oil, thyme, oregano, salt, and pepper. Pulse until smooth and creamy. Set aside.
3. Plug in the instant pot and press the "Saute" button. Melt the butter in the stainless steel insert and add asparagus. Cook for 3-4 minutes, stirring occasionally. Pour in the garlic sauce and stir well. Cook for 5 more minutes and turn off the pot.
4. Transfer all to a serving bowl and serve immediately.
5. Optionally, drizzle with some lemon juice for some extra taste.
6. Enjoy!

Per Serving:
(Calories 245 | Total Fats 20.7g | Net Carbs: 7.5g | Protein 6.2g | Fiber: 5.4g)

Cabbage Stew

(Total Time: 25 MIN | Serves: 4)

Ingredients:

- 2 cups purple cabbage, shredded
- 5 bacon slices, chopped
- 2 medium-sized celery stalks, chopped
- 1 medium-sized red bell pepper, chopped
- 2 cups vegetable stock
- 1 cup heavy cream
- ½ cup feta cheese, cubed
- 1 tbsp olive oil
- 1 tsp balsamic vinegar

Spices:
- 1 tsp sea salt
- ½ tsp cayenne pepper, ground
- ½ tsp dried thyme, ground
- ½ tsp garlic powder

Directions:

1. Plug in your instant pot and press the "Saute" button. Add bacon and cook for 3 minutes, or until crisp.
2. Add cabbage, celery, and red bell pepper. Sprinkle with salt, cayenne pepper, thyme, and garlic powder. Pour in the vegetable stock and heavy cream.
3. Securely lock the lid and set the steam release handle. Press the "Manual" button and set the timer for 15 minutes. Cook on "High" pressure.
4. When you hear the cooker's end signal, perform a quick pressure release by moving the valve to the "Venting" position.
5. Open the pot and stir in the feta cheese, olive oil, and vinegar. Press the "Saute" button and cook for 5 minutes more.
6. Turn off the pot and transfer all to a serving pot.
7. Enjoy!

Per Serving:
(Calories 338 | Total Fats 28.8g | Net Carbs: 5.7g | Protein 13.3g | Fiber: 2g)

Vegetables and Vegetarian Dishes

Creamy Zucchini Soup

(Total Time: 15 MIN | Serves: 4)

Ingredients:

- 4 medium-sized zucchinis, peeled and chopped
- 2 cups vegetable stock
- 2 garlic cloves, crushed
- 2 cups heavy cream
- 1 small onion, chopped
- 1 tbsp butter

Spices:
- 1 tsp sea salt
- ½ tsp dried oregano, ground
- ½ tsp black pepper, ground
- 1 tsp dried parsley, ground

Directions:

1. Plug in the instant pot and add butter to the stainless steel insert. Press the "Saute" button and melt, stirring gently with a wooden spatula.
2. Add onions, garlic, and chopped zucchinis. Cook for 3 minutes, stirring occasionally.
3. Pour in the vegetable broth and sprinkle with salt, oregano, pepper, and parsley. Stir well and lock the lid. Adjust the steam release handle and press the "Manual" button. Set the timer for 5 minutes and cook on "High" pressure.
4. When done, perform a quick release of the pressure by moving the valve to the "Venting" position.
5. Open the pot and transfer all to a serving dish. Optionally, sprinkle with some lemon juice.
6. Enjoy!

Per Serving:
(Calories 277 | Total Fats 25.5g | Net Carbs: 8.1g | Protein 4.2g | Fiber: 3g)

Vegetables and Vegetarian Dishes

Swiss Chard Leek Stir-Fry

(Total Time: 20 MIN | Serves: 4)

Ingredients:

- 2 cups Swiss chard, chopped
- 2 cups leeks, chopped
- 1 small onion, chopped
- 2 garlic cloves, finely chopped
- 1 tbsp olive oil
- ½ cup cream cheese, full-fat
- 2 tbsp Parmesan cheese, grated

Spices:
- ½ tsp black pepper, ground
- ¼ tsp cayenne pepper, ground
- 1 tsp pink Himalayan salt

Directions:

1. In a large colander, combine Swiss chard and leek. Rinse under cold running water and drain. Chop into small pieces and set aside.
2. Plug in the instant pot and add olive oil to the stainless steel insert. Press the "Saute" button and add onions and garlic. Cook for 5 minutes, or until the onions translucent.
3. Now, add greens and sprinkle with salt, pepper, and cayenne pepper. Stir-fry for 10-12 minutes.
4. Stir in the cream cheese and sprinkle all with parmesan. Continue to cook for 2-3 minutes more, stirring occasionally.
5. Transfer all to serving dish and enjoy!

Per Serving:
(Calories 195 | Total Fats 15.4g | Net Carbs: 8.81g | Protein 5.8g | Fiber: 1.6g)

Vegetables and Vegetarian Dishes

Creamy Bell Pepper Stew

(Total Time: 15 MIN | Serves: 4)

Ingredients:

- 2 large red bell peppers, chopped
- 1 medium-sized yellow bell pepper, chopped
- 1 medium-sized green bell pepper, chopped
- 1 medium-sized celery stalk, chopped
- 1 small red onion, chopped
- 2 tbsp butter
- 2 cups vegetable stock
- 1 cup heavy cream
- ½ cup cream cheese, full-fat

Spices:
- 1 tsp salt
- ½ tsp black pepper, ground
- 1 tsp dried parsley, ground
- ¼ tsp dried thyme, ground

Directions:

1. Plug in your instant pot and press the "Saute" button. Melt the butter in the stainless steel insert and add bell peppers, celery, and onions. Cook for 3-4 minutes, stirring occasionally.
2. Pour in the vegetable stock and heavy cream. Sprinkle with salt, pepper, parsley, and thyme. Give it a good stir and close the lid.
3. Set the steam release handle by moving the valve to the "Sealing" position. Press the "Manual" button and set the timer for 6 minutes. Cook on "High" pressure.
4. When done, perform a quick pressure release by turning the valve to the "Venting" position.
5. Open the pot and stir in the cream cheese. Let it chill for 10 minutes before serving.
6. Enjoy!

Per Serving:
(Calories 292 | Total Fats 27.3g | Net Carbs: 6.8g | Protein 4.4g | Fiber: 2.9g)

Vegetables and Vegetarian Dishes

Steamed Eggplant

(Total Time: 25 MIN| Serves: 3)

Ingredients:

- 1 eggplant, sliced into thin slices
- 4 garlic cloves, crushed
- 3 tbsp olive oil
- 1 tbsp butter
- 1 tbsp balsamic vinegar
- 2 tbsp Parmesan cheese, grated

Spices:
- 1 tsp salt
- ½ tsp black pepper, ground
- ¼ tsp onion powder

Directions:

1. Combine garlic, olive oil, balsamic vinegar, salt, pepper, and onion powder. Mix until well combined.
2. Place the sliced eggplant in a large bowl. Drizzle with previously prepared marinade and refrigerate for 20 minutes.
3. Plug in the instant pot and pour 1 cup of water in the stainless steel insert. Set the trivet on the bottom and place the steam basket on top. Place the eggplants in the steam basket and close the lid.
4. Set the steam release handle and press the "Steam" button. Set the timer for 15 minutes.
5. When done, perform a quick pressure release and open the pot.
6. Remove the steam basket and water from the pot. Clean and pat dry with a kitchen paper.
7. Press the "Saute" button and melt the butter in the stainless steel insert. Add eggplant and cook for 2 minutes. Now, sprinkle with parmesan cheese and cook until melts.
8. Turn off the pot and transfer to a serving plate.

Per Serving:
(Calories 231 | Total Fats 20.1g | Net Carbs: 5.5g | Protein 4.9g | Fiber: 5.6g)

Mushrooms with Asparagus

(Total Time: 15 MIN| Serves: 2)

Ingredients:

- 2 cups button mushrooms, chopped
- 1 cup asparagus, trimmed and chopped
- 1 small onion, chopped
- 2 garlic cloves, minced
- 2 tbsp olive oil
- 2 cups vegetable stock
- 2 oz mozzarella cheese

Spices:
- 1 tsp sea salt
- ½ tsp black pepper, ground
- ¼ tsp dried thyme, ground
- ½ tsp cayenne pepper, ground

Directions:

1. Plug in the instant pot and press the "Saute" button. Grease the stainless steel with olive oil and add button mushrooms and onions. Cook for 5 minutes, stirring occasionally. Sprinkle with some salt, pepper, and thyme.
2. Add chopped asparagus and pour in the vegetable stock. Sprinkle with cayenne pepper and lock the lid. Set the steam release handle by moving the valve to the "Sealing" position.
3. Set the timer for 5 minutes and cook on "High" pressure.
4. When you hear the cooker's end signal, perform a quick pressure release by moving the valve to the "Venting" position.
5. Open the pot. Using a large slotted spoon, transfer the mushrooms and asparagus to a serving plate.
6. Top with mozzarella cheese and serve immediately.

Per Serving:
(Calories 256 | Total Fats 19.6g | Net Carbs: 8g | Protein 12.8g | Fiber: 3.7g)

Spinach Cherry Tomato Hash

(Total Time: 15 MIN | Serves: 2)

Ingredients:

- 2 cups spinach, chopped
- 1 cup cherry tomatoes, halved
- 1 medium-sized red bell pepper, chopped
- 1 medium-sized onion, chopped
- 2 tbsp Greek yogurt, full-fat
- 1 tbsp fresh chives, finely chopped
- 3 tbsp butter
- ¼ cup cottage cheese

Spices:
- 1 tsp smoked paprika, ground
- 1 tsp cayenne pepper, ground
- 1 tsp salt
- ½ tsp garlic powder
- ½ tsp black pepper, ground

Directions:

1. Place spinach in a large colander. Rinse thoroughly under cold running water and drain. Chop into small pieces and set aside.
2. Plug in your instant pot and press the "Saute" button. Add butter and melt, stirring constantly with a wooden spatula.
3. Add spinach, leeks, tomatoes, bell pepper, and onions. Stir-fry for 5 minutes.
4. Sprinkle with smoked paprika, cayenne pepper, salt, garlic powder, and black pepper. Continue to cook for 5 more minutes.
5. Stir in the Greek yogurt and cook for about 2 more minutes.
6. Turn off the pot and transfer all to a serving plate. Top with cottage cheese and sprinkle with chives.
7. Serve immediately.

Per Serving:
(Calories 271 | Total Fats 19.2g | Net Carbs: 13.7g | Protein 9.9g | Fiber: 4.6g)

Vegetables and Vegetarian Dishes

Garlic Bok Choy

(Total Time: 20 MIN | Serves: 3)

Ingredients:

- 2 lbs bok choy, chopped
- 4 garlic cloves, crushed
- ½ cup sour cream
- ½ cup vegetable stock
- 1 small onion, chopped
- 2 tbsp olive oil

Spices:
- 1 tsp sea salt
- ½ tsp black pepper, ground
- ¼ tsp smoked paprika, ground

Directions:

1. Rinse the bok choy under cold running water. Drain and cut into bite-sized pieces. Set aside.
2. Plug in your instant pot and grease the stainless steel insert with olive oil. Press the "Saute" button and add onion and garlic. Stir-fry for 2-3 minutes, or until onions almost translucent.
3. Add book choy and cook for 2-3 minutes. Pour in the vegetable broth and sour cream. Stir well and bring it to a boil. Sprinkle with salt, pepper, and smoked paprika. Simmer for 5 more minutes.
4. Turn off the pot and transfer all to a serving dish.
5. Serve as a side dish in smaller portions or as a main dish.
6. Optionally, drizzle with some lemon juice or lemon vinegar.
7. Enjoy!

Per Serving:
(Calories 219 | Total Fats 18.1g | Net Carbs: 8.4g | Protein 6.4g | Fiber: 3.8g)

Vegetables and Vegetarian Dishes

Eggplant in Cream Chili Sauce

(Total Time: 20 MIN | Serves: 3)

Ingredients:

- 1 large eggplant, sliced
- 1 cup sour cream
- 3 garlic cloves, peeled
- 1 tbsp lemon juice, freshly squeezed
- 1 tbsp Greek yogurt
- 1 egg
- 1 tbsp olive oil

Spices:
- 1 tsp onion powder
- 1 tsp chili powder
- ¼ tsp dried oregano, ground
- ¼ tsp dried thyme, ground
- 1 tsp salt

Directions:

1. Combine sour cream, garlic, lemon juice, Greek yogurt, egg, and all spices in a food processor. Blend until smooth and creamy. Set aside.
2. Plug in the instant pot and grease the stainless steel insert with olive oil. Press the "Saute" button and spread the eggplant slices. Sprinkle with some salt and cook for 3-4 minutes on each side, or until lightly brown. Remove to a bowl and cover with a lid. Set aside.
3. Pour in the previously prepared mixture to the instant pot. Close the lid and adjust the steam release handle. Press the "Manual" button and set the timer for 3 minutes. Cook on "High" pressure.
4. When done, perform a quick pressure release by moving the valve to the "Venting" position and open the pot.
5. Drizzle the eggplants with the sauce and sprinkle with some green onions before serving.
6. Enjoy!

Per Serving:
(Calories 418 | Total Fats 34.1g | Net Carbs: 13.5g | Protein 10.4g | Fiber: 8.4g)

Vegetables and Vegetarian Dishes

Broccoli with Parsley Cheese

(Total Time: 20 MIN | Serves: 5)

Ingredients:

- 2 lbs broccoli, cut into stems
- 1 small onion, chopped
- 4 garlic cloves, peeled
- 1 cup cream cheese, full-fat
- ¼ cup fresh parsley, chopped
- ½ cup sour cream
- 1 tbsp lemon juice, freshly squeezed
- 1 tsp lemon zest, freshly grated
-
- Spices:
- 1 tsp salt
- 1 tsp Italian seasoning
- ¼ tsp cumin, ground
- 1 whole clove

Directions:

1. Plug in your instant pot and pour 4 cups of water in the stainless steel insert.
2. Add lemon juice, lemon zest, salt, Italian seasoning, and salt. Press the "Saute" button and bring it to a boil.
3. Now, add broccoli and close the lid. Set the steam release handle and press the "Manual" button. Set the timer for 5 minutes and cook on "High" pressure.
4. Meanwhile, combine cream cheese, parsley, sour cream, garlic, onions, and cumin in a food processor. Blend until smooth and creamy. Set aside.
5. When you hear the cooker's end signal, perform a quick pressure release and open the pot.
6. Transfer the broccoli to a serving plate and drizzle with previously prepared sauce.
7. Enjoy!

Per Serving:
(Calories 287 | Total Fats 9.8g | Net Carbs: 11.6g | Protein 9.8g | Fiber: 22g)

Vegetables and Vegetarian Dishes

Cauliflower Onion Hash

(Total Time: 20 MIN | Serves: 3)

Ingredients:

- 1 lb cauliflower, chopped
- 2 medium-sized onions, sliced
- 1 cup green cabbage, shredded
- 1 cup vegetable stock
- 2 tbsp olive oil
- ¼ cup parmesan cheese

Spices:
- 1 tsp salt
- ½ tsp dried thyme, ground
- ½ tsp smoked paprika, ground
- ¼ tsp black pepper, ground

Directions:

1. Plug in the instant pot and grease the stainless steel insert with olive oil. Press the "Saute" button and add cauliflower and onions. Sprinkle with salt, pepper, and thyme. Stir well and cook for 5 minutes.
2. Add cabbage and pour in the vegetables stock. Stir again and securely lock the lid. Set the steam release handle and press the "Manual" button. Set the timer for 8 minutes and cook on "High" pressure.
3. When you hear the cooker's end signal, perform a quick release of the pressure by moving the valve to the "Venting" position. Open the pot and stir in the thyme and smoked paprika.
4. Transfer all to a serving plate and sprinkle with parmesan cheese before serving.
5. Enjoy!

Per Serving:
(Calories 217 | Total Fats 13.7g | Net Carbs: 11.3g | Protein 10.3g | Fiber: 6.3g)

Brussels Sprouts with Mushrooms

(Total Time: 25 MIN | Serves: 4)

Ingredients:

- 1 lb Brussels sprouts, trimmed and halved
- 1 lb button mushrooms, sliced
- 1 medium-sized celery stalk, chopped
- 2 garlic cloves, crushed
- 1 tbsp fresh parsley, finely chopped
- 2 tbsp olive oil
- ¼ cup Greek yogurt, full-fat

Spices:
- 1 tsp ginger, freshly grated
- 1 tsp sea salt
- ½ tsp black pepper, ground
- ¼ tsp red chili flakes

Directions:

1. Plug in your instant pot and place the Brussels sprouts, mushrooms, and celery in the stainless steel insert. Sprinkle with some salt and pour water enough to cover all.
2. Securely lock the lid and set the steam release handle by turning the valve to the "Sealing" position.
3. Press the "Manual" button and set the timer for 10minutes. Cook on "High" pressure.
4. Meanwhile, in a medium-sized bowl, combine Greek yogurt, garlic, parsley, olive oil, and remaining spices. Mix until well combined and set aside.
5. When you hear the cooker's end signal, perform a quick pressure release by moving the valve to the "Venting" position.
6. Open the pot and stir in the yogurt mixture. Press the "Saute" button and cook for 5 more minutes.
7. Turn off the pot and transfer all to a serving bowl.
8. Enjoy!

Per Serving:
(Calories 145 | Total Fats 13.7g | Net Carbs: 10.7g | Protein 8.5g | Fiber: 5.7g)

Vegetables and Vegetarian Dishes

Spinach Pepper Stew

(Total Time: 15 MIN | Serves: 4)

Ingredients:

- 1 lb spinach, chopped
- 2 medium-sized bell peppers, chopped
- 1 cup fresh kale, chopped
- 1 cup vegetable stock
- 2 tbsp butter
- ¼ cup cream cheese, full-fat

Spices:
- 1 tsp salt
- ¼ tsp black pepper, ground
- ½ tsp red chili flakes
- ½ tsp dried mint, ground

Directions:

1. Plug in the instant pot and press the "Saute" button. Melt the butter in the stainless steel insert and add spinach, kale, and bell peppers. Sprinkle with salt, pepper, and red chili flakes. Stir well and cook for 5 minutes, or until greens are wilted.
2. Pour in the vegetables stock and give it a good stir. Securely lock the lid and set the steam release handle. Press the "Manual" button and set the timer for 8 minutes. Cook on "High" pressure.
3. When you hear the cooker's end signal, perform a quick release of the pressure by moving the valve to the "Venting" position. Open the pot and stir in the cream cheese and mint.
4. Transfer to a serving dish and optionally, add more salt to taste.
5. Serve warm.

Per Serving:
(Calories 209 | Total Fats 15.3g | Net Carbs: 9.8g | Protein 7.5g | Fiber: 5g)

Portobello Mushrooms in Lime Sauce

(Total Time: 15 MIN | Serves: 2)

Ingredients:

- 1 lb Portobello mushrooms, thinly sliced
- 4 garlic cloves, minced
- 1 small onion, chopped
- 1 whole lime, freshly juiced
- 1 tsp lime zest, freshly grated
- 1 cup heavy cream
- 1 tbsp butter

Spices:
- 1 tsp fresh ginger, grated
- 1 tsp sea salt
- 1 tsp apple cider vinegar
- 1 tsp black peppercorns, freshly ground

Directions:

1. In a food processor, combine garlic, onion, lime juice, heavy cream, ginger, apple cider vinegar, and black peppercorns. Process until smooth and creamy. Set aside.
2. Plug in your instant pot and press the "Saute" button. Add butter to the stainless steel insert and stir until melts.
3. Add sliced mushrooms and cook for 5 minutes, stirring occasionally. Remove the mushrooms to a plate and set aside.
4. Pour the lime sauce in the pot and bring it to a boil- Simmer for 4-5 minutes, stirring occasionally. Turn off the pot.
5. Place the mushrooms on a serving plate and drizzle with lime sauce. Sprinkle with lime zest and serve immediately.
6. Enjoy!

Per Serving:
(Calories 338 | Total Fats 28.1g | Net Carbs: 13.5g | Protein 8.8g | Fiber: 4.4g)

Vegetables and Vegetarian Dishes

Basil Pesto Zucchini

(Total Time: 20 MIN | Serves: 4)

Ingredients:

- 2 medium-sized zucchinis, thinly sliced
- 1 large red bell pepper, cut into strips
- 1 medium-sized eggplant, thinly sliced
- 1 cup mozzarella cheese
- 2 tbsp olive oil
- 1 tsp Italian seasoning
- 1 cup vegetable stock

For the basil pesto:
- 2 tbsp fresh basil, finely chopped
- 2 tbsp sour cream
- 3 tbsp olive oil
- ¼ tsp mustard seeds
- ½ tsp garlic powder
- 2 tsp balsamic vinegar
- ½ tsp black pepper, freshly ground

Directions:

1. Combine sliced zucchinis, stripped red bell pepper, and sliced eggplant in a large bowl. Drizzle with olive oil and Italian seasoning. Optionally, add a pinch of salt and mix well with your hands. Set aside.
2. Combine all pesto ingredients in a food processor and blend until smooth and creamy. Set aside.
3. Plug in the instant pot add vegetables in the stainless steel insert. Pour in the vegetable stock and close the lid. Adjust the steam release handle and press the "Manual" button. Set the timer for 8 minutes and cook on "High" pressure.
4. When done, perform a quick pressure release by moving the valve to the "Venting" position.
5. Open the pot and transfer the vegetables to a serving plate. Top with basil pesto and serve immediately.
6. Optionally, garnish with some fresh basil leaves and enjoy!

Per Serving:
(Calories 214 | Total Fats 17.4g | Net Carbs: 7.8g | Protein 5g | Fiber: 5.7g)

Vegetables and Vegetarian Dishes

Bell Peppers in Hot Sauce

(Total Time: 20 MIN | Serves: 4)

Ingredients:

- 1 medium-sized red bell pepper, chopped
- 1 medium-sized green bell pepper, chopped
- 1 medium-sized yellow bell pepper, chopped
- 1 medium-sized onion, sliced
- 1 small celery stalk, chopped
- 2 garlic cloves, finely chopped
- ½ cup tomatoes, diced
- 1 small chili pepper, finely chopped
- 2 tbsp olive oil
- 1 tbsp butter
- 2 tsp balsamic vinegar

Spices:
- ½ tsp salt
- ½ tsp black pepper, ground
- ¼ tsp ginger powder
- ¼ tsp dried thyme, ground

Directions:

1. In a food processor, combine tomatoes, garlic, chili pepper, olive oil, balsamic vinegar, and all spices. Blend until smooth and creamy. Set aside.
2. Plug in the instant pot and add butter to the stainless steel insert. Press the "Saute" button and melt.
3. Add bell peppers and onions. Stir-fry for 3-4 minutes, or until the onions translucent.
4. Add celery and pour in the previously blended mixture. Securely lock the lid and set the steam release handle. Press the "Manual" button and set the timer for 3 minutes. Cook on "High" pressure.
5. When you hear the cooker's end signal, perform a quick pressure release by moving the valve to the "Venting" position.
6. Open the pot and transfer all to a serving bowl. Optionally, top with some grated cheese such as parmesan or cheddar cheese.
7. Enjoy!

Per Serving:
(Calories 179 | Total Fats 13.6g | Net Carbs: 11.9g | Protein 2.2g | Fiber: 3.1g)

Instant Keto Vegetarian Pizza

(TotalTime: 1 HOUR 25 MIN| Serves: 4)

Ingredients:

- For the base:
- 1 cup almond flour
- 1/2 cup sunflower seeds, minced
- 1/2 cup sesame seeds, minced
- 1/4 cup flaxseed meal
- 1 1/2 tbsp psyllium husk
- 3 tbsp coconut oil, melted
- 2 cups hot water

For the topping:
- 1 small tomato, sliced
- ½ cup button mushrooms, sliced
- ½ cup mozzarella, sliced
- 1 tsp salt
- 2 tbsp olive oil
- ½ tsp dried oregano

Directions:

1. First, you'll have to prepare the crust. In a large bowl, combine together all dry crust ingredients and mix well. Add coconut oil and pour in two cups of boiling water. Let it sit for one hour.
2. Line a small baking pan with some parchment paper and add half of the crust mixture. Flatten the surface with your hands as evenly as possible and top with half of the toppings. The mixture will give you two small pizzas.
3. Loosely cover with aluminum foil and set aside.
4. Plug in the instant pot and set the trivet at the bottom of inner pot. Pour in one cup of water and place the pan on top.
5. Seal the lid and set the steam release handle to the "Sealing" position. Press the "Manual" button and cook for 5 minutes on high pressure.
6. When done, perform a quick pressure release and open the lid. Remove the pan from the pot and repeat the process with the remaining ingredietns.
7. Serve immediately.

Per Serving:

(Calories 233 | Total Fats: 19.2g | Net Carbs: 4.3g | Protein: 4.3g |Fiber: 8.5g)

Chapter 9
Stocks and Sauces

Stocks and Sauces

Basic Beef Stock

(TotalTime: 4 HOURS 30 MIN | Serves: 6)

Ingredients:

- 4 lbs beef marrow bones
- 1 tbsp lemon juice

Spices:
- 2 tsp salt
- 2 bay leaves
- ¼ cup fresh celery leaves, finely chopped

Directions:

1. Rinse well and drain the bones. Place in a deep bowl and cover with water. Drizzle with the lemon juice and soak for 30 minutes.
2. Transfer the bones along with the liquid to your instant pot. Add bay leaves and sprinkle with salt and celery.
3. Seal the lid and set the steam release handle to the "Sealing" position. Press the "Slow Cooker" button and set the timer for 4 hours on low heat.
4. When done, release the pressure naturally and open the lid. Optionally, sprinkle with some more lemon juice and strain the liquid.
5. Cool to a room temperature and refrigerate until use.

Per Serving:
(Calories 18 | Total Fats: 0.6g | Net Carbs: 0.2g | Protein: 2.8g | Fiber: 0.1g)

Stocks and Sauces

Lamb Stock with Celery

(TotalTime: 3 HOURS 15 MIN | Serves: 4)

Ingredients:

- 2 lbs lamb bones
- 2 large onions, sliced
- 2 celery stalks, chopped
- ½ cup celery leaves
- 2 tbsp apple cider vinegar

Spices:
- 1 tsp salt
- 1 tsp dried thyme

Directions:

1. Place the meat in the pot and pour in enough water to cover. Seal the lid and set the steam release handle to the "Sealing" position. Press the "Manual" button and set the timer for 15 minutes on high pressure.
2. When done, perform a quick pressure release and open the lid. Add the remaining ingredients and seal the lid again.
3. Set the steam release handle and press the "Slow Cooker" button. Set the timer for 3 hours on low pressure.
4. When done, release the pressure naturally. Remove the bones and keep the stock in the refrigerator until use.

Per Serving:
(Calories 42 | Total Fats: 0.6g | Net Carbs: 4.3g | Protein: 3.4g | Fiber: 1.4g)

Basic Beef Stock with Bay Leaves

(TotalTime: 1 HOUR 35 MIN | Serves: 8)

Ingredients:

- 4 lbs beef bones
- 3 tbsp red wine vinegar
- ½ cup celery stalk, finely chopped
- 5 garlic cloves, whole

Spices:
- 2 tsp pink Himalayan salt
- 1 tsp peppercorn
- ½ tsp dried basil

Directions:

1. Place the bones in a deep bowl and pour in enough water to cover. Add red wine vinegar and soak for one hour.
2. Plug in the instant pot and add bones along with water. Add garlic cloves, chopped celery, salt, peppercorn, and basil.
3. Seal the lid and set the steam release handle to the "Sealing" position. Press the "Manual" button and cook for 35 minutes on high pressure.
4. When done, release the pressure naturally and carefully open the lid. Season to taste and enjoy.

Per Serving:
(Calories 18 | Total Fats: 0.4g | Net Carbs: 0.5g | Protein: 2.3g | Fiber: 0.2g)

Spring Fish Stock

(Total Time: 30 MIN | Serves: 8)

Ingredients:

- 2 lbs sea bream, with bones
- 1 small leek, finely chopped
- 2 celery stalks, chopped
- 1 small zucchini, sliced
- 1 cup fresh celery leaves, finely chopped
- 2 tbsp lemon juice

Spices:
- 1 tbsp dried thyme
- 1 tbsp fresh rosemary, finely chopped
- 2 tsp salt

Directions:

1. Rinse and clean the fish. Drain in a large colander and transfer to the pot along with the remaining ingredients. Pour in enough water to cover and stir well.
2. Seal the lid and set the steam release handle to the "Sealing" position. Press the "Manual" button and set the timer for 20 minutes on high pressure.
3. When done, release the pressure naturally and open the lid. Optionally, sprinkle with some apple cider or freshly squeezed lemon juice.
4. Chill for a while and strain the liquid. Transfer to jars with tight lids and refrigerate until use.

Per Serving:
(Calories 31 | Total Fats: 1.1g | Net Carbs: 1.7g | Protein: 2.9g | Fiber: 0.6g)

Chicken Vegetable Stock

(TotalTime: 7 HOURS| Serves: 6)

Ingredients:

- 2 lbs chicken neck and backs, meat on
- 1 cup broccoli, chopped
- 1 cup artichoke, chopped
- 1 cup cherry tomatoes
- 1 cup spring onions, chopped
- 1 medium-sized celery stalk, chopped
- ½ cup dill, chopped
- 1 small onion, sliced
- 1 small carrot, sliced
- ½ cup apple cider vinegar

Spices:
- 2 tsp sea salt
- 1 tsp white pepper
- 2 tbsp dried celery

Directions:

1. Place the chicken in a deep pot and pour in enough water to cover and apple cider. Sprinkle with one teaspoon of salt and soak for one hour. When done, transfer to the pot.
2. Rinse and slice the vegetables. Place in the pot and season with the remaining salt, pepper, and celery. Optionally, add a couple of garlic cloves or season with some dried herbs like rosemary or thyme.
3. Seal the lid and set the steam release handle to the "Sealing" position. Press the "Slow Cooker" button and set the timer for 6 hours on low pressure.
4. When you hear the end signal, perform a quick pressure release and open the lid. Chill for a while and strain the liquid.

Per Serving:
(Calories 20 | Total Fats: 0.4g | Net Carbs: 2.1g | Protein: 1g | Fiber: 0.7g)

Lamb Ribs Stock

(Total Time: 40 MIN | Serves: 6)

Ingredients:

- 2 lbs lamb ribs, meat on
- 1 carrot, sliced
- 2 small onions, sliced
- 1 large tomato, whole
- 3 tbsp olive oil

Spices:
- 1 tsp sea salt
- 1 tsp black pepper, freshly ground
- 1 tbsp smoked paprika

Directions:

1. Rinse the lamb under cold running water and drain in a large colander. Chop in smaller pieces and place in the pot.
2. Pour in enough water to cover and season with salt. Seal the lid and set the steam release handle. Press the "Manual" button and cook for 20 minutes on high pressure.
3. When you hear the cooker's end signal, perform a quick release and open the lid. Add sliced carrot, onions, tomato, pepper, and smoked paprika.
4. Stir well and seal the lid again. Set the steam release handle to the sealing position and press the "Manual" button again. Continue to cook for 10 more minutes.
5. When done, release the pressure naturally and open the lid. Strain the liquid and stir in the olive oil.
6. Chill for a while and transfer to glass jars. Refrigerate until use.

Per Serving:
(Calories 77 | Total Fats: 7.5g | Net Carbs: 0.7g | Protein: 2.1g | Fiber: 0.6g)

Easy Chicken Stock

(TotalTime: 30 MIN | Serves: 4)

Ingredients:

- 2 lbs chicken neck and backs
- 2 chicken thighs, whole
- ½ cup fresh parsley, finely chopped

Spices:
- 2 tsp sea salt
- 1 tsp dried thyme
- 1 tsp peppercorn

Directions:

1. Rinse well the chicken and place in the pot. Pour in enough water to cover and stir in freshly chopped parsley. Optionally, add some finely chopped celery stalk and season with salt, thyme, and peppercorn.
2. Seal the lid and set the steam release handle to the "Sealing" position. Press the "Manual" button and set the timer for 25 minutes on high pressure.
3. When done, release the pressure naturally and open the lid. Chill for a while and then strain the stock.

Per Serving:
(Calories 12 | Total Fats: 0.6g | Net Carbs: 1g | Protein: 0.8g | Fiber: 0.3g)

Spicy Pepper Beef Stock

(Total Time: 40 MIN | Serves: 6)

Ingredients:

- 2 lbs beef bones
- 3 chili peppers, whole
- 4 garlic cloves, whole
- ¼ cup celery stalk, chopped
- ¼ cup celery leaves, chopped
- ¼ cup onions, chopped
- 3 tbsp red wine vinegar

Spices:
- 1 tsp salt
- 2 tsp chili pepper
- ½ tsp red pepper flakes

Directions:

1. Place the bones in the pot and pour in enough water to cover. Add vegetables and drizzle with red wine vinegar. Season with salt, chili pepper, and pepper flakes.
2. Stir well and seal the lid. Set the steam release handle to the "Sealing" position and press the "Manual" button. Set the timer for 35 minutes on high pressure.
3. When done, release the pressure naturally and open the lid. Stir well again and strain the liquid.
4. Chill for a while and refrigerate.

Per Serving:
(Calories 17 | Total Fats: 0.4g | Net Carbs: 0.8g | Protein: 2g | Fiber: 0.3g)

Ginger Chicken Stock

(Total Time: 25 MIN | Serves: 7)

Ingredients:

- 2 lbs chicken breast bones
- 1 medium-sized onion, sliced
- 1 small ginger knob
- 2 tbsp extra virgin olive oil
- 2 tbsp apple cider vinegar
- 1 tbsp freshly squeezed lemon juice
- 1 tbsp freshly grated lemon zest

Spices:
- 1 tsp sea salt
- 1 tsp black pepper, freshly ground

Directions:

1. Plug in the instant pot and press the "Saute" button. Grease the inner pot with olive oil and add onions. Cook for 3-4 minutes, stirring constantly. Now add chicken, lemon zest, and ginger. Pour in about one cup of water and give it a good stir. Simmer for 10-12 minutes. Place the bones in the pot and pour in one cup of water and apple cider vinegar. Sprinkle with one teaspoon of salt and press the "Saute" button. Bring it to a boil and gently simmer for 10-15 minutes. Make sure to skim of the foam that might appear on top.
2. Now press the "Cancel" button and add the remaining ingredients. Pour in 7 cups of water and seal the lid. Set the steam release handle to the "Sealing" position and press the "Manual" button. Set the timer for 12 minutes on high pressure.
3. When done, release the pressure naturally and open the lid. Chill for a while and strain the stock.
4. Optionally, sprinkle with some white pepper and refrigerate.

Per Serving:
(Calories 46 | Total Fats: 4.5g | Net Carbs: 1.1g | Protein: 0.7g | Fiber: 0.2g)

Sour Onion Sauce

(TotalTime: 15 MIN | Serves: 2)

Ingredients:

- 1 large onion, sliced
- 1 tbsp olive oil
- 1-2 tbsp apple cider vinegar
- 2 tsp almond flour
- 1 cup water or chicken stock

Spices:
- 1 tsp stevia powder
- 1 tsp cayenne pepper
- ¼ tsp salt

Directions:

1. Plug in the instant pot and press the "Saute" button. Heat up the olive oil and add onions. Sprinkle with salt and stevia and cook for 2-3 minutes, or until translucent.
2. Now add almond flour and give it a good stir. Continue to cook for one more minute and then add cayenne pepper. Pour in water or chicken stock and sprinkle with apple cider vinegar.
3. Bring it to a boil and press the "Cancel" button. Chill for a while and store until use.

Per Serving:
(Calories 108 | Total Fats: 8.4g | Net Carbs: 6g | Protein: 1.4g | Fiber: 2.1g)

Classic Bolognese

(TotalTime: 2 HOURS 20 MIN | Serves: 6)

Ingredients:

- 1 lb ground pork
- 10 oz ground beef
- ¼ cup celery stalks, chopped
- 1 onion, sliced
- 2 garlic cloves, crushed
- 2 tbsp parsley leaves
- 1 small chili pepper, sliced
- 6 tbsp tomato sauce, sugar-free
- ¼ cup balsamic vinegar
- 4 tbsp olive oil

Spices:
- 1 ½ tsp salt
- ½ tsp black pepper, freshly ground
- ½ tsp dried basil
- ½ tsp dried oregano

Directions:

1. Plug in the instant pot and press the "Saute" button. Grease the inner pot with olive oil and heat up. Add onions, garlic, chili pepper, and celery. Sprinkle with salt and cook for 5-6 minutes, stirring occasionally.
2. Now add the meat, tomato sauce, and red wine vinegar. Sprinkle with pepper, basil, and oregano. Stir well again and continue to cook for 5 minutes.
3. Finally, pour in 4 cups of water and sprinkle with parsley. Press the "Cancel" button and seal the lid.
4. Set the steam release handle to the "Sealing" position and press the "Slow Cooker" button. Set the timer for 2 hours.
5. When done, release the pressure naturally and open the lid. Serve immediately or store for later.

Per Serving:
(Calories 293 | Total Fats: 15g | Net Carbs: 2.5g | Protein: 34.7g | Fiber: 0.9g)

Sweet BBQ Sauce

(Total Time: 35 MIN | Serves: 4)

Ingredients:

- 2 lbs tomatoes, chopped
- 1 cup swerve
- 4 garlic cloves
- 3 tbsp apple cider vinegar
- ¼ cup soy sauce
- 2 tsp agar powder

Spices:
- 2 tsp salt
- ½ tsp cinnamon powder
- ½ tsp black pepper, freshly ground
- ½ tsp curry powder
- 2 cloves

Directions:

1. Place tomatoes in the pot and sprinkle with salt. Pour in 3 cups of water and seal the lid. Set the steam release handle to the "Sealing" position and press the "Manual" button.
2. Set the timer for 5 minutes.
3. When done, perform a quick pressure release and open the lid. Stir in apple cider, stevia, garlic, and cloves. Press the "Saute" button and bring it to a boil. Gently simmer for 15 minutes.
4. Finally, add soy sauce, agar powder, and the remaining spices. Continue to cook for 2-3 minutes, stirring constantly.
5. Press the "Cancel" button and chill for a while. Transfer the mixture to a food processor and process until smooth.

Per Serving:
(Calories 59 | Total Fats: 0.5g | Net Carbs: 8.9g | Protein: 3.3g | Fiber: 3.2g)

Tartare Sauce with Homemade Mayonnaise

(Total Time: 15 MIN | Serves: 6)

Ingredients:

For the mayonnaise:
- 4 large eggs
- 1 ½ cup heavy cream
- 2 tbsp apple cider vinegar
- 1 tsp Dijon mustard
- 1 garlic clove
- ¼ tsp pepper
- ¼ tsp sea salt

For the tartare:
- 1 garlic clove, crushed
- 2 tbsp olive oil
- ½ tsp Dijon mustard
- 1 tsp freshly squeezed lemon juice
- 1 tsp salted capers
- 3 pickles
- 1 cup homemade mayonnaise

Directions:

1. Plug in the instant pot and set the trivet at the bottom of the inner pot. Pour in one cup of water.
2. Place eggs in the steam basked and transfer to the pot. Seal the lid and set the steam release handle to the "Sealing" position.
3. Press the "Manual" button and set the timer for 4 minutes.
4. When done, perform a quick pressure release and open the lid. Remove the eggs and chill for a while.
5. Transfer eggs to a food processor along with other mayonnaise ingredients. Process until smooth. Set aside.
6. Now plug in the instant pot and grease the inner pot with olive oil. Add garlic and drizzle with lemon juice. Briefly cook – for one minute and press the "Cancel" button.
7. Stir in the remaining ingredients and add one cup of mayonnaise. Stir well and refrigerate until use.

Per Serving:
(Calories 198 | Total Fats: 19.2g | Net Carbs: 1.7g | Protein: 5g | Fiber: 0.5g)

Creamy Parsley Sauce

(TotalTime: 15 MIN | Serves: 5)

Ingredients:

- 2 cups fresh parsley, finely chopped
- 3 tbsp butter, unsalted
- 1 ½ cup whole milk
- 4 tbsp heavy cream
- 4 tbsp cream cheese
- 2 tbsp gorgonzola cheese
- ½ tsp agar powder

Spices:
- ½ tsp salt
- ½ tsp black pepper, freshly ground

Directions:

1. Plug in the instant pot and press the "Saute" button. Melt the butter in the inner pot and add cream cheese and gorgonzola cheese. Stir well and cook until the cheese melts. Now pour in the heavy cream and milk. Sprinkle with parsley and season with salt and pepper.
2. Stir well and season with salt and pepper. Cook for 2 minutes or until the sauce thickens.
3. Press the "Cancel" button and serve immediately.

Per Serving:
(Calories 198 | Total Fats: 17.9g | Net Carbs: 4.8g | Protein: 4.9g | Fiber: 1g)

Spinach Sauce with Milk

(TotalTime: 15 MIN | Serves: 4)

Ingredients:

- 4 cups spinach, chopped
- 2 tbsp almond flour
- ½ tsp agar powder
- 1 small onion, finely chopped
- 2 garlic cloves, crushed
- 1 ½ cup whole milk
- ¼ cup sour cream

Spices:
- ½ tsp white pepper
- ½ tsp sea salt

Directions:

1. Rinse well the spinach under cold running water and drain in a large colander. Place in the pot and add butter. Press the "Saute" button and give it a good stir. Cook until spinach has wilted.
2. Now add onions and garlic. Sprinkle with salt and pepper and cook for 2 minutes, stirring constantly.
3. Finally, pour in the milk and add sour cream, almond flour, and agar powder. Stir well and bring it to a boil. Cook for 2 minutes, stirring constantly.

Per Serving:
(Calories 123 | Total Fats: 7.8g | Net Carbs: 7.3g | Protein: 5.3g | Fiber: 1.6g)

Sour Garlic Sauce

(TotalTime: 15 MIN | Serves: 4)

Ingredients:

- 3 garlic cloves, crushed
- 1 ½ cup of milk
- 2 tbsp almond flour
- 2 tbsp butter
- 1 tsp apple cider vinegar

Spices:
- ¼ tsp dried thyme
- ¼ tsp garlic powder

Directions:

1. Grease the inner pot with butter and press the "Saute" button. Heat up and add garli. Sprinkle with thyme and garlic powder.
2. Cook for one minute and then add milk. Drizzle with apple cider vinegar and bring it to a boil.
3. Press the "Cancel" button and remove from the pot. Serve with meat.

Per Serving:
(Calories 121 | Total Fats: 9.3g | Net Carbs: 5.6g | Protein: 4g | Fiber: 0.4g)

Stocks and Sauces

Instant Pot Marinara

(TotalTime: 15 MIN| Serves: 5)

Ingredients:

- 4 large tomatoes, finely chopped
- 1 onion, finely chopped
- 3 garlic cloves, crushed
- 3 tbsp olive oil
- ¼ cup balsamic vinegar
- 1 celery stalk, chopped
- 2 tbsp Parmesan cheese

Spices:
- 1 tsp salt
- 1 tsp fresh basil, finely chopped
- 1 tsp tsp dried celery
- 1 bay leaf

Directions:

1. Plug in the instant pot and press the "Saute" button. Grease the inner pot with olive oil and heat up.
2. Add onions and cook for 5 minutes, stirring occasionally.
3. Now add garlic and continue to cook for another minute. Stir in celery stalk and tomatoes. Give it a good stir and then pour in the balsamic vinegar and 1 cup of water. Season with salt, basil, celery, and bay leaf.
4. Seal the lid and set the steam release handle to the "Sealing" position. Press the "Manual" button and set the timer for 7 minutes on high pressure.
5. When done, perform a quick pressure release and open the lid. Remove the bay leaf and chill for a while.
6. Transfer the mixture to a food processor and process until smooth. Refrigerate until use.

Per Serving:
(Calories 131 | Total Fats: 9.9g | Net Carbs: 6.4g | Protein: 3.5g | Fiber: 2.3g)

Stocks and Sauces

Butter Sauce with Green Peppers

(TotalTime: 20 MIN| Serves: 3)

Ingredients:

- 2 green bell peppers, chopped
- 2 tbsp almond flour
- ¼ cup whole milk
- ½ small onion, finely chopped
- 2 tbsp olive oil
- ¼ cup butter

Spices:
- ½ tsp salt
- ¼ tsp freshly ground black pepper
- ¼ tsp garlic powder
- ½ tsp dried basil

Directions:

1. Melt the butter on the "Saute" mode and add bell peppers and onions. Sprinkle with salt and cook until peppers have softened.
2. Now add olive oil and season with black pepper, garlic powder, and basil. Stir in almond flour and continue to cook for another minute.
3. Pour in the milk and give it a good stir. Bring it to a boil and press the "Cancel" button.
4. Remove the sauce from the pot and use immediately.

Per Serving:
(Calories 287 | Total Fats: 27.8g | Net Carbs: 7.4g | Protein: 2.8g |Fiber: 1.9g)

Tomato Onion Sauce

(TotalTime: 20 MIN | Serves: 8)

Ingredients:

- 2 large tomatoes, roughly chopped
- 1 cup tomato sauce, sugar-free
- 2 onions, chopped
- 2 garlic cloves, crushed
- 2 tbsp tomato paste
- 3 tbsp olive oil

Spices:
- 2 tsp stevia powder
- ½ tsp dried thyme
- 1 tsp salt

Directions:

1. Heat up the oil on the "Saute" mode. Add onions and garlic and sauté for 3-4 minutes.
2. Then add tomatoes and seasn with stevia, salt, and dried thyme. Pour in about ¼ cup of water and simmer until tomatoes have softened and most of the liquid has evaporated.
3. Stir in tomato paste and add tomato sauce. Give it a good stir and continue to cook for a couple of minutes more. Optionally, season with some more salt, thyme, or some other herbs of choice.

Per Serving:
(Calories 76 | Total Fats: 5.5g | Net Carbs: 5.2g | Protein: 1.3g | Fiber: 1.8g)

Dijon Sauce

(Total Time: 20 MIN | Serves: 4)

Ingredients:

- 1 cup heavy cream
- 2 tsp Dijon mustard
- ¼ cup feta cheese
- ¼ cup parmesan, freshly grated
- 2 tsp lemon juice, freshly squeezed
- 1 garlic clove, crushed
- 2 tbsp fresh parsley, finely chopped
- 2 tbsp olive oil

Spices:
- 1 tsp pink Himalayan salt
- ¼ tsp black pepper, freshly ground
- ½ tsp cayenne pepper

Directions:

1. Plug in the instant pot and press the "Saute" button. Grease the inner pot with olive oil and heat up. Add garlic and cook for one minute.
2. Now add heavy cream, cheese, and Dijon. Sprinkle with lemon juice and fresh parsley. Season with salt, pepper, and canyenne.
3. Give it a good stir and cook for 2-3 minutes.
4. Press the "Cancel" button and optionally transfer to a food processor. Process until completely smooth.
5. Serve.

Per Serving:
(Calories 215 | Total Fats: 21.7g | Net Carbs: 1.8g | Protein: 4.4g | Fiber: 0.2g)

Button Mushroom Sauce

(TotalTime: 10 MIN| Serves: 4)

Ingredients:

- 2 cups button mushrooms, sliced
- 1 cup heavy cream
- 3 tbsp sour cream
- 3 tbsp gorgonzola cheese
- 2 tbsp soy sauce
- 2 tbsp butter
- 1 tbsp sesame oil
- 2 tbsp Parmesan cheese, freshly grated
- 1 tsp agar powder

Spices:
- 1 tsp salt
- 1/3 tsp black pepper
- 1 tsp dried celery

Directions:

1. Melt the butter on the "Saute" mode and add mushrooms. Season with salt and pepper.
2. Give it a good stir and cook until the liquid from the mushrooms evaporates.
3. Njow add sour cream, gorgonzola cheese, and heavy cream. Sprinkle with dried celery and cook until cheese melts.
4. Finally, pour in the soy sauce and add sesame oil. Stir in agar powder and briefly cook – for another minute.
5. Press the "Cancel" button and remove the sauce from the pot.
6. Serve immediately.

Per Serving:
(Calories 265 | Total Fats: 26g | Net Carbs: 3.1g | Protein: 6.6g | Fiber: 0.7g)

Chapter 10

Desserts

Easy Almond Brownies

(TotalTime: 40 MIN | Serves: 6)

Ingredients:

- 2 large eggs
- ¾ cup swerve
- ½ cup almond flour
- ½ cup almonds, finely chopped
- 3 tsp baking powder
- ¼ cup coconut flour
- ½ cup whole milk
- ½ cup oil

Topping:
- ¾ cup milk
- ¾ cup swerve
- 2 oz unsweetened dark chocolate
- 4 tbsp butter

Directions:

1. In a large mixing bowl, combine together almond flour, coconut flour, baking powder, and swerve. Mix well and add eggs, one at the time, beating constantly with a paddle attachment on.
2. Now pour in the milk and oil. Continue to beat for 2-3 minutes, or until completely incporporated.
3. Lightly grease a small baking pan with some oil and line with some parchment paper. Dust with unsweetened cocoa powder.
4. Pour the mixture into the prepared baking pan and loosely cover with aluminum foil.
5. Plug in the instant pot and set the trivet at the bottom of the inner pot. Pour in one cup of water and place the pan on top.
6. Seal the lid and set the steam release handle. Press the "Manual" button and set the timer for 25 minutes on high pressure.
7. When done, perform a quick pressure relase and open the lid. Remove the pan from the pot and chill for a while.
8. Now press the "Saute" button and melt the butter. Stir in the butter and chocolate. Pour in the milk and bring it to a boil. Cook until all the chocolate has melted.
9. Pour the mixture over brownies and cool completely before slicing.

Per Serving:
(Calories 470 | Total Fats: 45.8g | Net Carbs: 5.8g | Protein: 6.7g | Fiber: 5g)

Desserts

Creamy Vanilla Cake

(TotalTime: 35 MIN| Serves: 8)

Ingredients:

For the crust:
- 5 eggs
- 2 ½ cups almond flour
- ¼ cup swerve
- 1 tbsp baking powder
- 3 tbsp coconut oil
- 4 tbsp cocoa powder, unsweetened
- ¼ cup milk

For the cream cheese layer:
- 2 cups mascarpone cheese
- ¼ cup whipped cream, unsweetened
- 2 tsp vanilla extract
- ¼ cup swerve

Directions:

1. Plug in the instant pot and position a trivet in the inner pot. Pour in one cup of water and set aside.
2. In a large mixing bowl, combine together almond flour, swerve, baking powder, and cocoa powder. Mix well and then add eggs, coconut oil, and milk. Using a hand mixer beat well on high speed. Pour the mixture into the lightly greased springform pan and wrap with some aluminum foil.
3. Place the pan on the trivet and seal the lid. Set the steam release handle to the "Sealing" position and press the "Manual" button. Set the timer for 15 minutes on high pressure.
4. When done, perform a quick pressure release and open the lid. Remove the pan from the pot and chill for a while.
5. Meanwhile, combine together mascarpone, whipped cream, vanilla extract, and swerve. Beat well with a hand mixer. Optionally, add some more sweetener or vanilla extract.
6. Pour the cream mixture over the chilled crust and flatten the surface with a kitchen spatula.
7. Refrigerate for at least two hours before serving.

Per Serving:
(Calories 266 | Total Fats: 21.7g | Net Carbs: 5g | Protein: 13.1g |Fiber: 1.8g)

Sweet Potato Cake

(TotalTime: 1 HOUR 30 MIN | Serves: 10)

Ingredients:

For the crust:
- 1 ½ cups of almond flour
- 3 tsp baking powder
- 1 tsp cinnamon powder
- ¼ cup finely chopped hazelnuts
- 3 large eggs
- ¾ cup coconut oil, melted
- ¾ cup swerve
- 1 tsp vanilla extract
- 1 medium-sized sweet potato, chopped
- 1 tbsp lemon zest

For the filling:
- 1 ½ cup cream cheese
- 1 tbsp coconut flour
- ½ tsp vanilla extract
- ¼ cup swerve

For the topping:
- ½ stick butter, unsalted
- ¼ cup almond flour
- ¼ cup swerve
- ½ tsp cinnamon powder

Directions:

1. First, prepare the topping. Plug in the instant pot and press the "Saute" button. Melt the butter in the inner pot and add swerve and cinnamon powder. Cook for 2-3 minutes, stirring constantly.
2. Now add flour and give it a good stir. Press the "Cancel" button and remove form the pot. Set aside.
3. Now, prepare the crust. Combine all dry ingredients in a large bowl and mix together. Add eggs, sweet potato, coconut oil, and vanilla powder. Transfer the mixture to a food processor and process until smooth. Set aside.
4. Line a small springform pan with some parchment paper and spray with a non-stick cooking spray. Add the crust mixture and flatten the surface as evenly as possible. Tightly wrap with aluminum foil and set aside.
5. Now, position a trivet at the bottom of the instant pot and pour in about one cup of water. Place the springform pan in the pot and seal the lid.
6. Set the steam release handle to the "Sealing" position and cook for 20 minutes on the "Manual" mode.
7. When done, perform a quick pressure release and open the lid. Carefully remove the springform pan from the pot and place on a wire rack to cool. Remove the aluminum foil and set aside.
8. Finally, prepare the filling. Combine the cream cheese with swerve, vanilla extract, and coconut flour. Using a hand mixer beat well on medium speed. If the mixture is too thick, add some unsweetend almond milk or sugar-free whipped cream.
9. Pour the mixture over the chilled crust and refrigerate for one hour.
10. Remove the cake from the refrigerator and top with the chilled cinnamon mixture.

Per Serving:
(Calories 384 | Total Fats: 38.2g | Net Carbs: 4.8g | Protein: 6.3g | Fiber: 1.8g)

Desserts

Mocha Brownies

(TotalTime: 45 MIN | Serves: 6)

Ingredients:

For the base:
- 6 eggs, separated
- 1 ½ cup swerve
- 1 ½ cups of almond flour
- 3 tbsp butter, unsalted
- 2 tsp baking powder
- ¼ tsp salt

For the topping:
- 5 egg yolks
- 1 ½ cup swerve or stevia crystal
- ¼ cup black coffee, unsweetened
- 2 butter sticks, unsalted

Directions:

1. Place egg whites in a large mixing bowl and beat on medium speed until light and fluffy. Add swerve, almond glour, melted butter, baking powder, and salt. Beat well on medium-high speed until completely incporporated.
2. Line a small cake pan with some parchment paper and add the batter. Tightly wrap with aluminum foil and set aside.
3. Plug in the instant pot and position a trivet at the bottom of the inner pot. Pour in some water and add the cake pan.
4. Securely seal the lid and set the steam release handle to the "Sealing" position. Press the "Manual" button and set the timer for 15 minutes on high pressure.
5. When done, perform a quick pressure release and open the lid. Remove the pan from the pot and set aside to cool.
6. Now place a steam basket in the stainless steel insert and pour in some more water. Set aside.
7. In a large mixing bowl, combine together the filling ingredients. With a whisking attachment on, beat well on medium-high speed for 2-3 minutes.
8. Pour the mixture into an oven-safe bowl and wrap with aluminum foil. Place the bowl in the steam basket and seal the lid.
9. Set the steam release handle and cook for 4 minutes on the "Manual" mode.
10. When you hear the cooker's end signal, perform a quick pressure release and open the lid. Remove the bowl from the pot and chill for a while.
11. Pour the mixture over the crust and cool to a room temperature. Refrigerate for at least an hour before serving.

Per Serving:
(Calories 236 | Total Fats: 21.1g | Net Carbs: 2.3g | Protein: 9.4g | Fiber: 0.8g)

Pumpkin Pie Bundt Cake

(TotalTime: 40 MIN | Serves: 5)

Ingredients:

- ¾ cup almond flour
- ¾ cup coconut flour
- 1 tsp baking soda
- ½ tsp baking powder
- ¾ cup swerve
- 2 tbsp coconut oil, melted
- ½ cup Greek yogurt
- ¼ cup pumpkin puree
- 1 large egg
- 1 tsp vanilla extract

Spices:
- ½ tsp salt
- 2 tsp pumpkin pie mix

Directions:

1. Grease a small bundt cake with some oil and set aside.
2. In a large mixing bowl, combine together almond flour, coconut flour, baking soda, baking powder, swerve, pumpkin spice pie, and salt. Stir well and add coconut oil, Greek yogurt, egg, and vanilla. With a paddle attachment on, beat well on high speed until fully incorporated.
3. Transfer the batter to the prepared bundt cake pan and tightly wrap with aluminum foil. Set aside.
4. Plug in the instant pot and set the trivet at the bottom of the inner pot. pour in about 2 cups of water and carefully place the bundt cake pan on top. Seal the lid and set the steam release handle to the "Sealing" position.
5. Press the "Manual" button and set the timer for 30 minutes on high pressure.
6. When done, perform a quick pressure release and open the lid.
7. Gently remove the pan from the pot and chill for a while before removing it from the pan.

Per Serving:
(Calories 145 | Total Fats: 9.8g | Net Carbs: 4.7g | Protein: 5.5g | Fiber: 4.4g)

Classic Keto Cheesecake

(Total Time: 2 HOURS 20 MIN | Serves: 8)

Ingredients:

- 1 cup almond flour
- ¼ cup flaxseed meal
- 6 large eggs, separated
- 4 tbsp coconut oil, melted
- 1 tbsp sesame seeds
- 2 tbsp almonds, finely chopped
- 1 tbsp peanut butter, melted
- ½ tsp salt
- 2 tsp stevia powder

For the topping:
- 3 cups Mascarpone
- 1 cup whipping cream, sugar-free
- ½ cup plain Greek yogurt
- ½ cup swerve
- 2 tsp vanilla extract

Directions:

1. Plug in the instant pot and position a trivet at the bottom of the inner pot. Pour in one cup of water and set aside.
2. Place egg wites in a large mixing bowl and add stevia. With a whisking attachment on, beat well on high speed.
3. Now add egg yolks, almond flour, flaxseed meal, and the remaining crust ingredients.
4. Using a paddle mixing attachment beat on medium speed until fully incorporated. Transfer the batter to lightly greased springform pan and set aside.
5. Now combine the cheese topping ingredients and beat with a hand mixer for 2-3 minutes.
6. Tightly wrap with aluminum foil and place in the pot. Seal the lid and set the steam release handle.
7. Press the "Slow Cooker" button and set the timer for 2 hours.
8. When done, perform a quick pressure release and open the lid. Carefully remove the pan and cool to a room temperature.
9. Transfer to the refrigerator and cool completely before serving.

Per Serving:
(Calories 397 | Total Fats: 32.5g | Net Carbs: 5.2g | Protein: 19.4g | Fiber: 1.8g)

Pecan Brownies

(TotalTime: 45 MIN | Serves: 6)

Ingredients:

- 4 tbsp butter
- 2 large eggs
- ½ cup almond flour
- 2 tsp baking powder
- 1/3 cup cocoa powder, unsweetened
- 1/3 cup swerve
- 4 tbsp dark chocolate chips, sugar-free
- 2 tbsp plain Greek yogurt
- ¼ cup pecans, finely chopped

Spices:
- 1 tsp vanilla extract
- ½ tsp cinnamon powder

Directions:

1. Line a small cake pan with some parchment paper and lightly coat with some cooking spray. Set asde.
2. Plug in the instant pot and position a trivet at the bottom of the stainless steel insert. Pour in two cups of water and set aisde.
3. In a large mixing bowl, combine together butter, eggs, and swerve. With a paddle attachment on, beat well for 2-3 minutes on medium-high speed.
4. Gradually add almond flour and baking powder, beating constantly.
5. Finally, add the remaining ingredients and beat until completely incorporated. Transfer the dough to a clean work surface and shape approximately bite-size balls. Transfer half of the balls to the prepared cake pan and gently flatten each with the palm of your hand.
6. Loosely cover the pan with some aluminum foil and place in the pot. Seal the lid and set the steam release handle to the "Sealing" position. Press the "Manual" button and set the timer for 15 minutes on high pressure.
7. When done, perform a quick pressure release and open the lid. Remove the pan from the pot and transfer cookies to a wire rack to cool.
8. Repeat the process with the remaining dough.

Per Serving:
(Calories 202 | Total Fats: 19.5g | Net Carbs: 2.8g | Protein: 5.1g | Fiber: 3g)

Simple Vanilla and Chocolate Chips Cake

(TotalTime: 30 MIN| Serves: 8)

Ingredients:

- 1 cup almond flour
- ¼ cup cocoa powder, unsweetened
- ¼ cup swerve
- 4 large eggs
- ¼ cup coconut oil, melted
- ¼ cup chocolate chips, unsweetened
- 2 tbsp finely chopped almonds, optional

Spices:
- 2 tsp vanilla extract
- ½ tsp nutmeg

Directions:

1. Plug in the instant pot and set the trivet at the bottom of the inner pot. Pour in two cups of water and set aside.
2. Line a small springform pan with some parchment paper and dust with some cocoa powder.
3. Combine the ingredients in a large mixing bowl and beat well on medium-high speed. Pour the batter into the prepared springform and shake a couple of times to flatten the surface.
4. Tightly wrap the cake with a large piece of aluminum foil and place in the pot. Seal the lid and set the steam release handle.
5. Press the "Manual" button and set the timer for 20 minutes on high pressure.
6. When done, perform a quick pressure release and open the lid. Carefully remove the pan from the pot and set aside to cool for a while.
7. Refrigerate for about an hour before serving.

Per Serving:
(Calories 158 | Total Fats: 13.6g | Net Carbs: 4.3g | Protein: 5.1g | Fiber: 1.6g)

Chocolate Brownies with Orange Glaze

(Total Time: 45 MIN | Serves: 8)

Ingredients:

- 1 ½ cups of almond flour
- 3 large eggs
- ¼ cup coconut oil, softened
- ¼ cup cocoa powder, unsweetened
- 2 tsp baking soda
- ¼ cup swerve
- ¼ cup unsweetened almond milk
- 1 tsp vanilla extract

For the glaze:
- 1 cup unsweetened dark chocolate, 80% cocoa
- 3 tbsp coconut oil
- 2 tbsp orange zest
- 1 tsp orange extract

Directions:

1. Combine together all dry ingredients. Mix well and add eggs, one at the time, mixing constantly on medium speed. Finally, add almond milk, coconut oil, and vanilla extract.
2. Continue to mix until completely incporporated. Set aside.
3. Grease a small cake pan with some coconut oil and lightly dust with unsweetened cocoa powder. Add the prepared bater and loosely cover with aluminum foil.
4. Plug in the instant pot and set the trivet at the bottom of the inner pot. Pour in one cup of water and place the cake pan on top.
5. Seal the lid and set the steam release handle to the "Sealing" position. Press the "Manual" button and set the timer for 25 minutes on high pressure.
6. When done, perform a quick pressure release and open the lid. Carefully remove the pan from the pot and cool for a while.
7. Meanwhile, press the "Saute" button and add chocolate and coconut oil. Gently melt, stirring constantly.
8. When the chocolate has completely melted, press the "Cancel" button and remove the mixture from the pot.
9. Brush the chilled brownies with the orange mixture and cool well before slicing.

Per Serving:
(Calories 230 | Total Fats: 21.5g | Net Carbs: 7g | Protein: 4.5g | Fiber: 2.1g)

Desserts

Quick Rum Cocoa Truffles

(TotalTime: 10 MIN | Serves: 10)

Ingredients:

- 1 cup shredded coconut
- 1 cup dark chocolate chips, sugar-free
- 3 tbsp butter
- 1 cup heavy cream
- 4 tbsp swerve
- 4 tbsp cocoa powder, unsweetened

Spices:
- 1 tsp rum extract
- 1 tsp lime zest, freshly grated

Directions:

1. Plug in the instant pot and add butter to the stainless steel insert. Press the "Saute" button and melt, stirring with a wooden spatula.
2. When melted, add chocolate chips, heavy cream, swerve, and rum extract. Stir well and cook for 3 minutes, stirring constantly.
3. Turn off the pot and stir in the shredded coconut. Let it chill for a while.
4. Transfer to an air-tight container and refrigerate for 1 hour. Use an ice cream scoop to form the truffles. Roll each in cocoa and serve immediately.
5. Enjoy!

Per Serving:
(Calories 245 | Total Fats: 22.1g | Net Carbs: 12.3g | Protein: 2.6g | Fiber: 2.3g)

Raspberry Cheesecake

(TotalTime: 2 HOURS 20 MIN | Serves: 6)

Ingredients:

- 1 cup almond flour
- ¼ cup sunflower seeds
- ¼ cup almond butter
- 5 eggs
- 3 tsp stevia powder
- ¼ tsp salt

For the filling:
- 3 cups cream cheese
- ½ cup heavy cream
- 1 tsp agar powder
- 4 tbsp stevia powder
- 1 tsp raspberry extract

Directions:

1. Line a fitting springform pan with some parchment paper and grease the walls with some cooking spray. Set aside.
2. In a large mixing bowl, combine almond flour, sunflower seeds, stevia, and salt. Using a spatula, mix until well incorporated. Set aside.
3. In a separate bowl, combine eggs and butter. With a whisking attachment on, beat with a hand mixer for 3-4 minutes.
4. Now, pour egg mixture into dry ingredients. With a paddle attachment on, beat until combined.
5. Transfer the dough mixture to the springform pan and spread evenly. Set aside.
6. In a large mixing bowl, combine all filing ingredients and beat for 3 minutes with a hand mixer. Pour the filling over the crust.
7. Plug in the instant pot and pour 1 cup of water in the stainless steel insert. Set the trivet on the bottom. Place the springform pan on the top and seal the lid. Adjust the steam release handle and press the "Slow Cooker" button. Set the timer for 2 hours and cook on "Low" pressure.
8. When you hear the cooker's end signal, perform a quick pressure release and open the pot. Transfer the pan to a wire rack and let it chill for at least an hour. Refrigerate for 30 minutes before serving.
9. Optionally, top with some fresh raspberries.

Per Serving:

(Calories 535 | Total Fats: 51.4g | Net Carbs: 4.5g | Protein: 15.1g | Fiber: 0.7g)

Desserts

Chocolate Cake

(TotalTime: 1 HOUR 40 MIN | Serves: 6)

Ingredients:

- 1 ½ cups of almond flour
- 1 tsp baking powder
- 1/3 cup swerve
- 2 large eggs
- 4 tbsp almond butter
- 2 tbsp almonds, roughly chopped
- ½ tsp salt
- 1 tsp vanilla extract

For the filling:
- ½ cup raw cocoa, unsweetened
- 1 cup Mascarpone cheese
- ¼ cup whipping cream
- 1 tbsp sour cream
- 3 tsp stevia powder

Directions:

1. In a large mixing bowl, combine almond flour, baking powder, salt, swerve, and almonds. Mix until combined and set aside.
2. In a separate bowl, whisk together eggs, butter, and vanilla extract.
3. Now, combine wet and dry ingredients and mix until well incorporated. Set aside.
4. Grease a fitting springform pan with some cooking spray. Spread the previously prepared mixture evenly and press with your palm to form a crust.
5. Plug in the instant pot and pour in 1 cup of water. Set the trivet on the bottom and place the pan on top. Tighly wrap the top of the pan with some aluminum foil. Close the lid and adjust the steam release handle. Press the "Manual" button and set the timer for 20 minutes. Cook on "High" pressure.
6. When done, open the pot and let it chill completely.
7. Meanwhile, prepare the filling. Combine all ingredients in a large bowl. With a whisking attachment on, whisk until creamy and smooth.
8. Pour the the filling mixture over the cust. Add ½ cup of water to the pot and return the pan to the trivet. Close the lid and adjust the steam release handle. Press the "Slow Cooker" mode and set the timer for 1 hour.
9. When done, open the pot and transfer the pan to a wire rack. Cool to a room temperature and refrigerate for 20-30 minutes before serving.
10. Optionally, sprinkle with some raw cocoa.
11. Enjoy!

Per Serving:
(Calories 250 | Total Fats: 20.3g | Net Carbs: 5.7g | Protein: 12.4g | Fiber: 4.2g)

Desserts

Coconut Cocoa Brownies

(Total Time: 1 HOUR 40 MIN| Serves: 6)

Ingredients:

- ½ cup shredded coconut
- ½ cup almond flour
- 1 cup cream cheese
- 4 tbsp coconut oil
- 2 tbsp swerve
- 2 tsp baking powder
- 4 tbsp raw cocoa, unsweetened

Spices:
- 1 tsp vanilla extract
- ½ tsp cinnamon, ground

Directions:

1. In a large mixing bowl, combine shredded coconut, almond flour, swerve, baking powder, and cocoa. Stir well until combined.
2. Now, add cream cheese and coconut oil. Using a hand mixer, beat until all well incorporated. Add vanilla extract and cinnamon and beat again for a minute. Set aside.
3. Pour 1 cup of water in the stainless steel insert of your instant pot. Position a trivet on the bottom. Line a fitting springform pan with a parchment paper and pour in the prepared mixture. Gently spread with a spatula and flatten the surface.
4. Set the pan on top a trivet and close the lid. Adjust the steam release handle and press the "Manual" button. Set the timer for 30 minutes and cook on "High" pressure.
5. When done, perform a quick release of the pressure by moving the valve to the "Venting" position.
6. Open the pot and let it chill to a room temperature. Cut into brownies and serve immediately.
7. Refrigerate up to 3 days.

Per Serving:
(Calories 260 | Total Fats: 26.4g | Net Carbs: 3.3g | Protein: 4.3g |Fiber: 2g)

Orange Lime Pudding

(Total Time: 10 MIN | Serves: 4)

Ingredients:

- ¼ cup almond milk, unsweetened
- 1 tsp agar powder
- ¼ cup coconut cream
- ¼ cup whipping cream
- 1 tbsp stevia powder
- 1 tbsp coconut oil

Spices:
- 1 tsp orange extract
- 1 tsp lime zest, freshly grated

Directions:

1. Plug in your instant pot and place coconut oil in the stainless steel insert. Press the "Saute" button and gently stir with a wooden spatula.
2. When melted, add almond milk, coconut cream, and whipping cream. Bring it to a light simmer, stirring constantly.
3. Stir in the stevia powder, agar powder, and orange extract. Cook for another 2-3 minutes, stirring constantly.
4. Turn off the pot and and pour the pudding into serving bowls or ramekins immediately.
5. Let it cool to a room temperature. Sprinkle with lime zest and refrigerate for 1 hour before serving.
6. Enjoy!

Per Serving:
(Calories 155 | Total Fats: 12.3g | Net Carbs: 10.7 | Protein: 0.7g | Fiber: 0.5g)

Almond Cocoa Spread

(Total Time: 15 MIN | Serves: 3)

Ingredients:

- 1 cup almonds
- 2 tbsp walnuts
- ¼ cup unsweetened cocoa powder
- ¼ cup coconut cream
- 2 tbsp stevia powder
- 4 tbsp coconut oil

Spices:
- 1 tsp vanilla extract
- ¼ tsp nutmeg, ground

Directions:

1. Combine almonds and walnuts in a food processor. Pulse until minced. Add coconut oil and pulse again for 1 minute. Transfer to a large bowl and stir in the stevia powder, vanilla extract, and nutmeg. Set aside.
2. Plug in your instant pot and pour the coconut cream in the stainless steel insert. Heat up over the "Saute" button and then add almond mixture. Stir in the cocoa, nutmeg, and vanilla extract.
3. Cook for 5 minutes, stirring occasionally.
4. Turn off the pot and let it chill to a room temperature. Store the spread in an air-tight container or a mason jar.
5. Refrigerate for 20 minutes before serving.
6. Optionally, add some lemon juice for zesty aroma.
7. Enjoy!

Per Serving:
(Calories 439 | Total Fats: 42.9g | Net Carbs: 5.4g | Protein: 9.8g | Fiber: 7.2g)

Desserts

Chia Vanilla Custard

(Total Time: 50 MIN | Serves: 4)

Ingredients:

- ¼ cup whole milk
- 1 cup heavy cream
- 5 large eggs
- 2 tbsp stevia powder
- ½ tsp agar powder
- 2 tbsp chia seeds

Spices:
- 1 tsp vanilla extract
- ¼ tsp cinnamon, ground

Directions:

1. In a large bowl, combine milk, heavy cream, eggs, stevia powder, agar powder, and chia seeds. Using a hand mixer, beat until well incorporated and creamy. Stir in the vanilla extract and beat for a minute more.
2. Pour the mixture into ramekins. Wrap the top of each ramekin with aluminum foil and set aside.
3. Plug in the instant pot and pour 1 cup of water in the stainless steel insert. Position a trivet on the bottom and place the ramekins on top.
4. Close the lid and adjust the steam release handle. Press the "Slow Cooker" mode and set the timer for 40 minutes.
5. When done perform a quick pressure release by moving the valve to the "Venting" position.
6. Open the pot and carefully remove the ramekins using oven mitts. Let it cool to a room temperature and then refrigerate for at least 20 minutes before serving.
7. Enjoy!

Per Serving:
(Calories 243 | Total Fats: 20.2g | Net Carbs: 2.7g | Protein: 10.3g | Fiber: 2.8g)

Walnut Pumpkin Mug Cake

(Total Time: 50 MIN | Serves: 2)

Ingredients:

- ½ cup almond flour
- 1 tbsp almonds, roughly chopped
- 1 tbsp walnuts, roughly chopped
- 1 tbsp chia seeds
- 1 tbsp pumpkin seeds
- 1 tbsp coconut oil, melted
- 1 tsp baking powder

Spices:
- ¼ tsp salt
- 2 tsp stevia powder
- ¼ tsp apple pie spice mix

Directions:

1. Combine almond flour, almonds, walnuts, chia seeds, pumpkin seeds, and baking powder in a large mixing bowl. Add melted coconut oil, stevia powder, and apple pie spice mix. Mix until well incorporated.
2. Pour the mixture into oven safe mugs and optionally, top with some dark chocolate chips.
3. Plug in the instant pot and pour 1 cup of water in the stainless steel insert. Place the trivet on the bottom and set the mugs on the top. Securely lock the lid and adjust the steam release handle. Press the "Manual" button and se the timer for 2 minutes on "High" pressure.
4. When you hear the cooker's end signal, perform a quick pressure release and open the pot. Carefully remove mugs from the pot and let it chill for 10 minutes before serving. Optionally, top with some extra pumpkin seeds.
5. Enjoy!

Per Serving:
(Calories 363 | Total Fats: 30.2g | Net Carbs: 6.2g | Protein: 11g | Fiber: 8.7g)

Chocolate Cake with Vanilla Glaze

(Total Time: 50 MIN | Serves: 6)

Ingredients:

- ½ cup almond flour
- 4 tbsp butter
- 3 tbsp stevia powder
- 5 large egg yolks
- 1 tsp agar powder
- ½ tsp salt
- 2 tbsp cocoa powder
- 1 tsp chocolate extract, unsweetened

For the glaze:
- 1 cup Mascarpone cheese
- 5 large egg whites
- 2 tbsp swerve
- 2 tsp vanilla extract
- Dark chocolate chips, optional

Directions:

1. Plug in the instant pot and pour 1 cup of water in the stainless steel insert. Line a fitting springform pan with some parchment paper and set aside.
2. In a large mixing bowl, combine egg yolks and butter. Beat with a hand mixer for 2-3 minutes, or until well combined. Add stevia, agar powder, salt, and cocoa, Beat again for 2 minutes. Finally, add almond flour and beat again until fully combined.
3. Pour the mixture in the springform pan and gently flatten the surface with a spatula.
4. Set the trivet on the bottom of your pot and place the pan on the top. Close the lid and adjust the steam release handle. Press the "Manual" button and set the timer for 40 minutes. Cook on "High" pressure.
5. Meanwhile, combine all glaze ingredients and remaining egg whites in a large mixing bowl. Beat until well combined and set aside.
6. When you hear the cooker's end signal, perform a quick pressure release and open the pot. Transfer the pan to a wire rack and let it cool for 10 minutes.
7. Top the cake with glaze and spread evenly. Add ½ cup of water to the pot and return the pan on top of the trivet. Close the lid and adjust the steam release handle. Cook for 1 minutes on the "Manual" mode.
8. When done, perform a quick pressure release and open the pot.
9. Chill to a room temperature and refrigerate for 20 minutes before serving.
10. Optionally, top with some dark chocolate chips for some extra flavor.

Per Serving:
(Calories 263 | Total Fats: 21.5g | Net Carbs: 3.6g | Protein: 12.3g | Fiber: 1.6g)

Rum Truffles

(Total Time: 50 MIN | Serves: 5)

Ingredients:

- ½ cup dark chocolate chips, melted
- 1 cup heavy cream
- ¼ cup granulated stevia
- ¼ tsp xanthan gum
- 3 egg yolks
- ½ cup whipped cream

Spices:
- ½ tsp rum extract
- ¼ tsp cinnamon, ground
- ½ tsp stevia powder

Directions:

1. In a mixing bowl, combine egg yolks, granulated stevia, and xathan gum. Using a hand mixer, beat until well incorporated. Add heavy cream, melted chocolate chips, rum extract, cinnamon, and stevia powder. Beat for 1 more minute and then pour into oven-safe ramekins. Wrap the top of each ramekin with aluminum foil and set aside.
2. Plug in your instant pot and pour 1 cup of water in the stainless steel insert. Position a trivet on the bottom and place ramekins on top. Close the lid and adjust the steam release handle. Press the "Manual" button and set the timer for 30 minutes. Cook on "High" pressure.
3. When you hear the cooker's end signal, release the pressure naturally. Open the pot and top with whipped cream and powdered stevia before serving.
4. Enjoy!

Per Serving:
(Calories 208 | Total Fats: 18.5g | Net Carbs: 9.4g | Protein: 3.2g | Fiber: 0.1g)

Desserts

Mint Cake

(Total Time: 60 MIN | Serves: 8)

Ingredients:

For the layers:
- 1 cup almond flour
- 1 cup coconut flour
- 1 tbsp stevia powder
- ¼ cup whole milk
- 3 tbsp butter
- 5 large eggs
- 1 tsp vanilla extract
- ½ tsp salt

For the filling:
- ¼ cup butter
- ½ cup cream cheese
- 2 tsp stevia powder
- 1 tsp mint extract

Directions:

1. In a large mixing bowl, combine almond flour, coconut flour, stevia powder, and salt. Mix until combined and set aside.
2. In a separate bowl, combine eggs, butter, milk, and vanilla extract. Using a hand mixer, beat until fluffy and then gradually add to dry ingredients. Mix until all well incorporated. Set aside.
3. In another bowl, combine all filling ingredients. With a paddle attachment on, beat until well combined and set aside.
4. Pour 1 cup of water in the stainless steel of your instant pot. Line a fitting springform pan with some parchment paper. Set the trivet on the bottom of the pot and place the pan on top. Pour half of the layer mixture in the pan and close the lid. Adjust the steam release handle and press the "Manual" button. Set the timer for 20 minutes and cook on "High" pressure,
5. When you hear the cooker's end signal, perform a quick pressure release and open the pot. Transfer the layer to a wire rack to cool. Repeat the process with the remaining mixture.
6. When the second layer is done, spread the filling over and top with the remaining layer. Close the lid of your pot and adjust the steam release handle. Press the "Manual" button and set the timer for 5 minutes on "High" pressure.
7. When done, perform a quick pressure release and open the pot.
8. Chill to a room temperature before serving and optionally, garnish with some fresh mint.

Per Serving:
(Calories 398 | Total Fats: 33.8g | Net Carbs: 6.6g | Protein: 10.5g | Fiber: 7.5g)

Vanilla Cherry Panna Cotta

(Total Time: 15 MIN | Serves: 2)

Ingredients:

For the vanilla layer:
- 1 cup heavy whipping cream
- 2 tbsp whole milk
- 1 tsp agar powder
- ½ tsp vanilla extract
- 1 tbsp walnuts, roughly chopped

For the cherry layer:
- 1 cup heavy whipping cream
- 1 tsp agar powder
- 1 tbsp almonds, roughly chopped
- 2 tsp cherry extract

Directions:

1. Plug in the instant pot and combine all vanilla layer ingredients in the stainless steel insert. Press the "Saute" button and stir constantly. Bring it to a light simmer and then press "Cancel" button. Transfer to a large bowl and set aside.
2. Clean the pot and pat-dry with a kitchen paper. Now, add all cherry layer ingredients and stir well. Again, bring it to a light simmer, stirring constantly.
3. Pour about ½-inch thick vanilla layer in a medium-sized glass. Now, add the second layer of the cherry mixture. Repeat the process until you have used both mixtures.
4. Optionally, garnish with some fresh mint and refrigerate for at least 1 hour before serving.
5. Enjoy!

Per Serving:
(Calories 467 | Total Fats: 48.7g | Net Carbs: 4.6g | Protein: 4.5g | Fiber: 0.8g)

Mocha Pots de Creme

(Total Time: 25 MIN| Serves: 4)

Ingredients:

- 2 large eggs, separated
- 1 cup coconut milk, full-fat
- ¾ cup heavy cream
- 2 tbsp cocoa powder, unsweetened
- 3 tbsp brewed espresso
- 3 tbsp stevia powder

Spices:
- ¼ tsp salt
- 1 tsp vanilla extract

Directions:

1. In a small bowl, whisk together eggs, cocoa powder, espresso, stevia powder, vanilla, and salt. Set aside.
2. Plug in the instant pot and press the "Saute" button. Pour in the coconut milk and heavy cream. Give it a good stir and warm up.
3. Press the "Cancel" button and slowly pour the warm milk mixture over the egg mixture, whisking constantly.
4. Divide the mixture between 4 ramekins and loosely cover with aluminum foil.
5. Position a trivet at the bottom of your pot and pour in 2 cups of water. Gently place the ramekins on top and seal the lid.
6. Set the steam release handle to the "Sealing" position and press the "Manual" button.
7. Cook for 15 minutes.
8. When done, perform a quick pressure release and open the lid. Remove the ramekins and transfer to a wire rack. Cool to a room temperature and then refrigerate for about an hour.

Per Serving:
(Calories 257 | Total Fats: 25.5g | Net Carbs: 3.5g | Protein: 5.5g | Fiber: 2.1g)

Lemon Cake with Berry Syrup

(Total Time: 45 MIN | Serves: 8)

Ingredients:

For the cake:
- 3 cups almond flour
- 3 tbsp stevia powder
- ¼ cup coconut milk, full-fat
- 1 tbsp coconut cream
- ¼ cup butter, softened
- 5 large eggs
- ¼ tsp salt
- 3 tsp baking powder
- 2 tsp lemon extract

For the syrup:
- ¼ cup raspberries
- ¼ cup blueberries
- 1 tbsp lemon juice, freshly squeeze
- ¼ cup granulated stevia

Directions:

1. In a large mixing bowl, combine together almond flour, stevia powder, baking powder, and salt.
2. Mix well and add eggs, one at the time, beating constantly.
3. Now add coconut milk, coconut cream, butter, and lemon extract. Using a paddle attachment beat for 3 minutes on medium speed.
4. Grease a small cake pan with some oil and line with parchment paper. Pour the mixture in it and tightly wrap with aluminum foil.
5. Plug in the instant pot and set the trivet at the bottom of the inner pot. Place the cake pan on top and pour in one cup of water.
6. Seal the lid and set the steam release handle to the "Sealing" position. Press the "Manual" button and cook for 25 minutes.
7. When done, perform a quick pressure release and open the lid. Carefully remove the pan and set aside.
8. Now press the "Saute" button. Add berries and pour in one cup of water and granulated stevia. Gently simmer for 5-6 minutes, stirring constantly.
9. Finally, add agar powder and give it a good stir. Cook until the mixture thickens.
10. Pour the syrup over chilled cake and refrigerate for 2 hours before serving.

Per Serving:
(Calories 186 | Total Fats: 16g | Net Carbs: 3.8g | Protein: 6.4g | Fiber: 1.3g)

Desserts

Easy Rum Cheesecake

(Total Time: 30 MIN| Serves: 10)

Ingredients:

- 2 cups almond flour
- 4 large eggs, separated
- ¼ cup coconut cream
- 2 tbsp almond butter
- ¼ cup cocoa powder, unsweetened
- ¼ cup swerve
- 3 tsp baking powder
- 3 cups Mascarpone
- 1 cup plain Greek yogurt
- 2-3 drops stevia

Spices:
- 2 tsp rum extract
- ½ tsp cinnamon powder

Directions:

1. Plug in the instant pot and position a trivet. Pour in one cup of water in the stainless steel insert and set aside.
2. Beat egg whites and swerve with a hand mixer until light foam appears. Add egg yolks, coconut cream, almond butter, baking powder, and cocoa powder, beating constantly.
3. Finally, add almond flour and continue to beat until completely combined.
4. Pour the mixture into lightly greased cake pan and cook for 15 minutes on the "Manual" mode.
5. When done, perform a quick pressure release and open the lid. Remove the cake from the pan and cool for a while.
6. Now combine Mascarpone and Greek yogurt. Add rum extract, cinnamon powder, and stevia. Using a hand mixer, mix well until completely combined.
7. Pour the mixture over the crust and refrigerate for a couple of hours before slicing.

Per Serving:
(Calories 247 | Total Fats: 18.1g | Net Carbs: 5.6g | Protein: 15.6g | Fiber: 1.7g)

Chapter 11
Conclusion

Conclusion

Well health food enthusiasts, that's it! You now have everything you need to embark on your nourishing Ketogenic adventure using your tried and true old pal, the Instant Pot™! These recipes are just the beginning of your wellness journey, and there are no limits to the endless possibilities your Instant Pot™ can whip up with your Ketogenic diet!

By now, you've probably learned that your Instant Pot™ is designed to help you make far more than just homestyle baked beans like your grandma's pressure cooker. From healthy soups and appetizers to main dishes and desserts, your Instant Pot™ was designed to tackle it all! The best part? Your Instant Pot™ is every chef's best friend since it is made of stainless steel that intentionally cuts out harmful chemicals, leaving only the delicious flavors of your wholesome ingredients.

Whether you are a seasoned Ketogenic eater or you are trying out this health-conscious diet for the first time, you now hold a complete guide to mastering the art of the Ketogenic Diet in a fraction of the time. Before you head out to the farmer's market and start chopping up veggies, we want to share some of our favorite tips and tricks for getting the most out of your Instant Pot™ and taking full advantage of the amazing new diet you've just started!

Ketogenic Eating On-the-Go

Unlike those fad diets you've seen advertised on TV, the Ketogenic Diet was created with busy people in mind. Whether you're grabbing a quick bite in between meetings, enjoying a healthy snack while shuffling your kids back and forth from soccer practice, or just trying to fit in a little home-style cooking into your routine, the Ketogenic Diet was designed to accommodate even the most hectic of schedules. So, how you may ask?

Well, for starters, there is no need for pre-portioned or frozen meals like other diets on the market. Sure, it's easy to eat well when you're confined to the contents of your freezer, but that leaves most of us hanging whenever we venture beyond the homestead. After all, can you really schlep those packaged meals with on-the-go when you're miles away from a microwave? We didn't think so!

Since the Ketogenic Diet promotes weight loss through your body's own natural process of breaking down fats, you won't start craving those quick pick-me-up's that become somewhat of a survival tool with other diets. At the end of the day, sticking to the Ketogenic Diet creates a healthy lifestyle (not just a fad eating trend) and can re-program your body to crave nourishing, wholesome ingredients instead of quick-processing sugars or carbohydrates.

When you learn to love organic and healthy foods like those found in the Ketogenic Diet, you can learn to choose these foods when you're out and about as well! Whether you're meeting your girlfriends for appetizers after work or picking up a quick bite during your lunch break, you'll be surprised how many healthy options are out there when you start looking!

Want to take your newfound love of the Ketogenic Diet with you on-the-go? Well, you've come to the right place because that brings us to our next tip...

The Ultimate Guide to Meal Prepping

Ask any fitness buff about their secret to staying ripped, and we bet that they will all answer with the same sound advice: meal prepping. The key to sticking with a diet and transforming eating habits into an oops-proof lifestyle is simple: you need access to hearty, wholesome foods 24/7!

This is where your Instant Pot™ truly comes in handy, fellow chefs! By far, one of the biggest perks of Instant Pot™ cooking is the ability to prepare delicious meals in bulk without wasting hours upon hours in the kitchen. How does this fit with your new diet? Put it this way, there are no excuses for skipping on Ketogenic eating when you can bring your latest Instant Pot™ creations with you to work, the neighborhood potluck, or anywhere else your busy life may take you!

Ready to get started? Check out our tried and true guide to meal prepping so you can enjoy the benefits of the Ketogenic Diet anytime, anywhere!

- Food Storage. You have your cookbook, organic ingredients, and Instant Pot™...now what?! Well, you're going to need a place to store all of that delicious food and containers to help you bring everything with you on-the-go. We recommend adding the following to your Ketogenic arsenal:

    o Leak-proof food storage containers in a variety of sizes (preferably glass to avoid those harmful chemicals found in plastic!);
    o Reusable storage bags; and
    o Eco-friendly food storage wraps (these are usually made of a cloth treated in beeswax and can be reused over and over again!).

- Prep Station. Make room for at least one week's worth of meals by clearing off a little space on your kitchen counter, coffee table; you name it! You won't need a ton of space, just enough to line your containers up in a neat little row (or two!) so you can prep like a well-oiled machine.

- A Little Time. This is our favorite part! No need to carve out an entire chunk of your day (or even a few hours), but you will want to set aside a designated time each week that is dedicated to food prep. We recommend taking advantage of your Sunday morning or afternoon; in no time at all, this will become one of your favorite weekly rituals!

- A Fun Lunch Bag or Tote! Pick a color, pattern, and style that you love to pack everything in each day. The more you love it, the more likely you are to bring your Ketogenic meals with you (and the less likely you are to walk out of the house realizing you forgot your lunch on the counter...again...for the third time this week!).

The Family Ketogenic Diet

Another thing we love about the Ketogenic Diet? It's perfect for the whole family! No matter how many people you have in your tribe, this healthy lifestyle is for everyone. After all, a family that eats together stays together!

Do you have little ones or picky eaters? No problem! Most of the recipes in this cookbook are healthy adaptations of the go-to meals your family already knows and loves. In fact, by substituting just a few ingredients, you may just fool those picky eaters into going carb-free without even knowing it...

Another bonus of bringing the whole family in on the Ketogenic fun? Support! Accountability and support are some of the most important factors in the success of a new healthy lifestyle, and having your family's seal of approval will make your success that much easier to attain. When you're all in on the fun, you won't have to worry about being tempted by one person's love of fried chicken or fast food burgers, and you will have the added bonus of creating a healthy, sustainable lifestyle for your entire family for years to come.

The Instant Pot + Ketogenic Eating: Endless Possibilities!

We've said it before, and we'll say it again: your Instant Pot™ was made to compliment the Ketogenic Diet! Whether you're trying out a new cuisine for the first time, treating your guests to a unique dessert, or preparing a nourishing soup for your sick kiddos on a cold winter day, your Instant Pot™ was designed to take the lead!

The more you use your Instant Pot™ and try out the recipes in this cookbook, the more comfort you'll gain in trying innovative recipes of your own! The same goes for Ketogenic eating; the longer you commit to this healthy lifestyle, the easier it will be to notice all of the options you have available at your disposal within this awesome way of eating!

Final Thoughts

Ketogenic eating is one of the fastest-growing diets in the world, and it's easy to understand why. From weight loss to increased energy and every health benefit in between, it's no wonder that this instinctual diet is taking the world by storm. Well, just like the Ketogenic Diet has become an overnight sensation, so has the Instant Pot™! Together, these two make one mean, green, wellness machine, and are your ticket to the healthy lifestyle you've always wanted.

Want to make the most of the recipes in this cookbook? Shop organic, locally-grown ingredients from your neighborhood farmer's market or small grocer! These ingredients are pesticide-free and typically come from the freshest farms around, so your recipes will always taste their very best! An added bonus? Shopping locally supports the farmers in your community while reducing environmental harms and promoting long-lasting sustainability.

Happy Cooking!

Made in the USA
San Bernardino, CA
25 April 2018